Forgo
Roo

Karol Kolbusz

ISBN: 9781790805228

Cover art: *Two Men Contemplating the Moon* by Caspar David Friedrich.

www.forgottenroots.wordpress.com

DEDICATION

The present work is dedicated to those who seek direction, hope, and inspiration in their wanderings throughout the dark labyrinths of modernity. May the light of Tradition guide them.

TABLE OF CONTENTS

23   On Indifference   85

     Summary   87

     Appendix A –   89
     How to Meditate

     Appendix B –   90
     Establishing
     Sacred Space

     Appendix C –   91
     Recommended
     Cultural Works

ACKNOWLEDGMENTS

The author would like to express his heartfelt gratitude to Ryan Dziadowiec for proofreading the entire text and suggesting additions and modifications.

INTRODUCTION

The following work is a compilation of my philosophical essays. The topics discussed in these writings stem chiefly from my reflections upon the spiritual condition of the European peoples in our present century. It is beyond any question that the modern world is a very sad place. Millions of people are suffering from depression, anxiety, hopelessness, and a lack of higher ideals in life. I believe that these problems indicate that we have lost our way on the path of civilizational progress, and that the very foundations upon which modernity is built are weak, rotten, and in urgent need of repair.

The purpose of this work is threefold: to examine these issues, to find possible explanations for the current spiritual crisis, and to put forward both short-term coping strategies and long-term solutions that could resolve it. The modern man has been severed from his own cultural and spiritual roots and I believe that we need to return to the old ways of our ancestors. Although traditional Indo-European philosophy and spirituality are the cornerstones of this book, indicating my desire for preserving the presented points of view, it does not aim to promote any political ideology. Every genuine seeker of knowledge and inspiration, regardless of his or her opinions, is therefore welcome to read my essays.

The poetic threads interwoven with the main body of the work serve the function of introducing my readers to a certain atmosphere and mood. Many of them have been (loosely or directly) inspired by my friends, people that I like and respect. The essays can be read selectively, though full comprehension and appreciation may require reading them all in the originally intended order. At the very end, I have included a list of recommended books, films, music, and visual artists. I hope you will find my recommendations useful in your cultural journeys.

ON PROGRESS

What Westeners call civilization, the others would call barbarity, because it is precisely lacking in the essential, that is to say a principle of a higher order.
– René Guénon[1]

The warm light of the March sun was shining through the gaps in the high, white clouds. An old man was standing in a place where, many years ago, there used to be a beautiful rural park and a playground. He remembered how every afternoon of the pale spring he would see children and teenagers joyously playing together and riding their bikes. As soon as the sun sank down below the horizon, the shadows would creep out and cover the park with a shroud of tranquillity. Now, a huge shopping centre stands there, bustling with activity, yet lifeless. The old grove of magnificent oak trees was cut down and the playground is no more. The youth are nowhere to be seen. Due to universal access to the Internet, their socialization is no longer limited to the playgrounds and parks of real life. Such is the nature of progress – it promises us artificial paradises of convenience, concrete, and plastic, but at the same time it conceals or destroys what is simple, direct, and organic.

***

The modern man is enamoured with the notion of indefinite progress. First of all, he is being told that he should take pride in the sophisticated technological advancements of our times. It is beyond any question that they have made our life easier, more convenient, and gave us opportunities unimaginable to the so-called primitive peoples. In my opinion, technological progress is not inherently a curse, as long as it is moderate, just like in the Classical Antiquity. The smart use of fire, wheel, nail, soap, compass, and paper contributed to the betterment of mankind. However, the disadvantages of unlimited progress in this field have outweighed the benefits in the last few centuries with the invention of technologies such as the steam engine, electricity, the telephone, and the internal combustion engine. Decades later, owing to the extensive use of television, mobile phones, and the Internet, we have only become lazier and lazier, more dependent on modern facilities, or in other words – tamed by the very same tools we have created in order to control our natural environment. We have replaced the strength of our muscles with mechanical tools and the brilliant capabilities of our brains with computers. Millions of trees and hectares of

---

1   R. Guénon, *East and West* (Hillsdale, NY: Sophia Perennis, 2001), p. 25.

ancient groves have been chopped down to clear the way for urbanization and industrial expansion. Never before in the history of the world have we witnessed such enormous environmental destruction of our blue planet.

Interestingly enough, in our current age, the primary motivation behind the endless pursuit of new technological advancements is not curiosity or willingness to improve the material condition of mankind. These are merely justifications given to the public. In reality, the producers of thousands of new gadgets every new year are driven by nothing but sheer greed. They are experts at creating artificial needs and duping consumers into believing that they must satisfy these needs at all costs. The modern man, trapped in the vicious circle of consumerism, has been manipulated to prioritize money-making and compulsive shopping over spending time with family members, celebrating traditions, cultivating health of the body and the soul, and strengthening connection with nature and the soil. There is nothing wrong with accumulating wealth, though, provided that it is used for noble purposes and not used as a key to the hellish gate of hedonistic pleasures. Unfortunately, it is the latter case that is prevalent in the modern world. We can conclude that with every technological novelty we are being thrown deeper and deeper into the poisoned wells of comfort and hedonism, at the significant expense of regression in the realm of spirituality. A valid argument against further technological progression is that the time between each new advancement decreases exponentially, thus giving people less and less time to consider the long-term implications of embracing the latest technologies. For example, the Internet has only existed for a few decades, and we still do not thoroughly understand how its daily usage can affect our mental and physical health.

Another blatantly false idea permeating the minds of our contemporaries is that the liberation of mankind from the snares of religious dogmatism and parochial attitudes has unlocked the gates of earthly paradises. It is commonly said that we are an inch away from achieving global happiness and peace. Those who set the modern world in motion are trying to convince us that we need to put aside (an ill-defined) hatred, and spread the gospel of love, peace, equality, democracy, solidarity, and tolerance. Chanted by the adversaries of Tradition, these empty slogans are in fact used as a justification for further enslavement of all peoples on Earth. The evangelists of progress have subtly tricked the modern man into believing that drowning in the pleasures of matter, worshipping gold, and rejecting the oppressive burden of spiritual authority and tradition will eventually eliminate all the pain and misery in this world. However, their optimistic prognoses have proven incorrect, as the desacralization of society has only made people more unhappy, lost, and depressed than ever before. Even today we can still find many individuals who believe that we are living in the age of greatest prosperity yet. In their arrogance, in spite of all the data that proves them wrong, they hold an erroneous view that our digital century is the best era in the history of mankind.

The notion of linear, uninterrupted progress in all aspects of human life is but a modern anomaly, unknown to the ancients. If we closely examine the perception of time and history in many of the Indo-European cultures, we will find a common belief in the cyclical stages of gradual devolution from the primordial, spiritual state of harmony with the divine. In his poem *Works and Days*, the Greek poet Hesiod wrote about the five successive ages of mankind. Their names corresponded with metals (with the exception of the Heroic Age). The Roman poet Ovid offered a similar account in *Metamorphoses*. In the Vedic tradition, the four world ages are called *yugas*. In the following paragraphs we are going to analyse each *yuga* in detail. But before we do so, we have to define the concept of *dharma*, which is essential for the full comprehension of the doctrine of downward progression over the ages.

Dharma can be understood as a cosmic law, with neither beginning nor end (thus it is eternal), which permeates and applies to all animate beings and inanimate objects in the universe. It is a supra-individual, metaphysical order that sets the physical world in a state of balance and harmony, protecting it from forces of chaos and dissolution. The concept of *dharma* stands in direct opposition to the current materialistic paradigm in science, according to which the universe is a mechanism devoid of any inherent meaning and purpose. The consequence of the latter worldview is ethical relativism and rejection of the notion that metaphysical principles and laws form the basis of reality. From such a limited point of view, we are born as mere pieces of flesh and bones that are left clueless and helpless in the face of the vast universe. *Dharma*, on the other hand, is a holistic natural law based on the premise that the universe is an extremely intelligent design rooted in transcendence. Many of the ancient civilizations, and particularly those of Indo-European origin, were *dharmic* in nature – meaning that all aspects of social life (religion, politics, science, law, literature, war, agriculture etc.) within them were constructed in consonance with *dharma*. Due to obvious racial, cultural, and linguistic differences, this universal law manifested itself in a slightly divergent way in each civilization. There was a time on Earth, however, when people across Europe and Asia were ruled by virtuous kings whose reign was strengthened by this primordial, sacred law. Before the advent of Abrahamic religions (Judaism, Christianity, Islam), one could hardly find a single war that was declared because of religious differences between the two conflicting parties. Such was the omnipresence of *dharma*. In the old Irish book of Leinster, we can read the following instructions left for the High King of Ireland:

Let him magnify the truth, it will magnify him.

Let him strengthen truth, it will strengthen him.

Let him guard truth, it will guard him.

Let him exalt truth, it will exalt him.

For so long as he guards truth, good shall not fail him and his rule

shall not perish.

For it is through the ruler's truth mighty armies of invaders are drawn

back into enemy territory.

Through the ruler's truth every law is glorious and every vessel full

in his lands.[2]

In this context truth is synonymous with *dharma*. As long as the king fulfils his duties in accordance with the natural law, his kingdom will flourish, both materially and spiritually. The purpose of ancestral traditions, transmitted either orally or through scriptures, was to remind people how to live a virtuous life in harmony with these universal principles.

According to the doctrine of the four cyclic ages, in each successive *yuga* one can observe a gradual decline of *dharma*, manifested by a decrease in knowledge, virtue, and health. In the Vedic tradition, *dharma* is figuratively depicted as a four-legged bull. The four legs symbolize virtues of austerity, cleanliness, compassion, and truthfulness. With every successive age, the bull loses one of its legs. In the Golden Age of humanity, also known as Satya Yuga ("Age of Truth"), there was no disease and the average life span was very high. People during that era, profoundly and effortlessly connected with the divine, led virtuous, peaceful, and happy lives. The first decline came with the advent of the Silver Age, known in Sanskrit as Treta Yuga ("Threefold Age"). The positive qualities characteristic to the previous era were diminished. Arguments and conflicts

---

2   *Book of Leinster*, quoted in: P. Berresford Ellis, *The Druids* (London: Constable, 1994), p. 169.

arose, people grew more materialistic and less concerned about religion. The art of agriculture was invented; men began to exploit the soil and nature in general. In the Bronze Age, parallel to the Vedic Dvapara Yuga ("Twofold Age"), there was an even greater decline in the moral and physical condition of humanity. People during this epoch were very warlike, competitive, deceitful, and attached to the pleasures of matter. Out of the four pillars of *dharma*, only two remained: compassion and truthfulness. The age in which we are currently living is known as Kali Yuga ("Age of Kali", Kali being the name of a demon), comparable with the Iron Age in the Graeco-Roman tradition.

Let us examine what are some of the most visible symptoms of Kali Yuga. In today's world, using vulgar, insulting, and sexualized language is a common social norm, not just a rare exception. A minor disagreement can incite people to jump to each other's throats, as well as to cancel solemn promises and friendships. Sociopathy, wickedness, and nihilism are spreading like a plague. It is so hard to find authentically religious individuals. The majority either does not believe in anything (with the sole exception of frenetic money-making and idolatric consumerism) or is falsely pious, indulging in degeneracy behind the façade of externally-projected religiosity. Marketing experts, cult leaders, New Age frauds, and hollow celebrities prey on people's misery and gullibility, duping them into buying products they don't need. Cultural heritage is no longer a refreshing well of wisdom and timeless inspiration, but something that can be commercialized and turned into a profitable fashion. An example of such trend is the growing interest in the Norse mythology and the Vikings, which is being exploited by those who want to make money from it. National leaders are not concerned about protecting their fellow compatriots, but rather plunder them through excessive taxation and undesirable laws. Modern art is tasteless and devoid of any transcendental meaning. It reflects the climate of spiritual degeneration in society. Last but not least, there are currently no social and political institutions grounded in a higher, spiritual tradition that could legitimate their power. In conclusion, what we witness today is the reversal of *dharma* in every single aspect of human life.

Contrary to what some misinformed individuals tend to think, the doctrine of the four cyclic ages does not imply fatalism and passive submission to the cosmic laws. The popular sentiment that we can do nothing about the current situation is false. Kali Yuga, the age of greatest decay and degeneracy, is actually the perfect time for heroes. It is still possible to arrange our lives in such a way that the poisonous trends of modernity do not compromise our inner constitution. Attaining peace and common understanding in the Golden Age was effortless, but it is now that we are in most desperate need of exceptionally talented, courageous, and noble-hearted defenders of *dharma*. How can they successfully oppose modernity? First of all, such individuals must accept reality as it is, without false hopes and delusions. We have to realize that today, as we speak, things are going downhill. The truth about the modern world is bitter (many politicians are deliberately trying to hide it from us), but it is necessary to acknowledge it if we want to achieve something meaningful. Secondly, we need to acquire proper self-knowledge, identify our weaknesses and improve ourselves accordingly. How can we change the world if we don't even know what kind of inner forces drive our actions? To begin making progress in this area, I would recommend studying ancient Greek and Roman philosophy, coupled with daily meditation. For example, the writings of the Stoics are good for self-improvement, while Plato's dialogues can sharpen our intellect. Secondly, let us not forget about keeping our bodies in good shape and health. Thirdly, it is crucial to ground our lives in authentic spiritual tradition. Sadly, due to the effect of time and the destructive impact of Abrahamic religions, many beliefs of the ancient Indo-Europeans (especially in Europe) are now partially lost to us. However, thanks to the tireless efforts of scholars and archaeologists, every new year brings advancement in this field. We can practice spirituality not only by the means of widening our understanding of ancient scriptures, performing sacrifice and praying to the gods, but also through vigorous and mindful action in the world. Finding the practical application of the *dharmic* laws certainly appeals to the active mind of the European man, though we must remember not to neglect the equally important former aspect of spirituality. More information on these three steps can be found in the subsequent essays.

Everyone must find their own path, as people have different talents and capabilities. My book is intended to act as a manual for those individuals who genuinely wish to make a real change in the world and who want to know how to defend themselves against the omnipresent corruption and decay. Although I humbly recognize that my work is certainly not an exhaustive study of the topics in question, it is written with the intention to inspire my readers to protest against the ongoing crisis of modernity by taking appropriate and decisive action.

***

It was a gloomy November afternoon. Dark clouds hung over the bleak grey hills. An elderly Danish woman was raking fallen leaves in the garden behind her cottage. She wore a brown kerchief about her grey hair. A short walk down the road from her garden there was an apple orchard in which a young girl was picking up the autumnal windfalls lying on the cold, damp ground. The cool air flushed her small, graceful hands. A little while later, both the woman and the girl came back to the cottage. The apples from the orchard were used to make a warm fruit beverage. They sat by the windowsill, slowly sipping the comforting liquid warmth inside their glasses. And then the rain came, blurring the sombre scenery of leafless trees and empty fields. In spite of the ubiquitous gloom that fell upon the hills, a single patch of celestial blueness, peering timidly through the ocean of grey, brought a promise of spring and rebirth.

Such is the nature of the eternal natural way reflected in our ancestral traditions. The concentrated efforts of those who wish to turn *dharma* upside down remain fruitless, for the ever-victorious Sun of Truth cannot be ultimately concealed, no matter how many times it is beclouded with lies, perversion, and devolution. It has always been and will ever be, so long as the world turns.

ON ENTHUSIASM

The Greeks have given us one of the most beautiful words of our language, the word "enthusiasm" – a God within. The grandeur of the acts of men are measured by the inspiration from which they spring. Happy is he who bears a God within.
– Louis Pasteur

It is so hard to find genuine joy and excitement in the modern world. Let us take an imaginary trip to a nearby city. What do we see? The streets are filled with numb, characterless faces that reflect neither sadness nor joy. In overcrowded trams and buses, people are coming home from joyless, purposeless jobs. If they ever feel enthusiasm, they feel an alienated form of it, ignited through the artificial joys of watching team sports, eating tasty food, shopping or waiting for a new season of their favourite TV show. It is often repeated that we live in exciting and colourful times, but what does this really mean? It means that we are continually bombarded and flooded with millions of useless, brain-muddling pieces of propaganda that appeal to the lowest instincts in man.

The word "enthusiasm" originates from the ancient Greek *énthous*, which means "possessed or inspired by a god". In the traditional world, nearly every act of artistic creativity drew inspiration from what is divine and sacred. The most beautiful and visually stimulating paintings and sculptures were directly inspired by religion and mythology (with very few exceptions). Whether we look at the majestic faces of Greek gods sculpted by Phidias, Emil Doepler's epic illustrations of Norse deities, or dream-like depictions of Aryan Hyperborea masterfully crafted by Vsevolod Ivanov, we can feel that these artists were guided by something higher and more powerful than themselves. Contrarily, what can we expect from art produced in a godless, utterly materialistic world? Ugliness; moral and aesthetic turpitude embodying the sheer, perpetual emptiness of the modern man. The soullessness of contemporary art cannot arouse real enthusiasm in our hearts, nor can it enhance our best qualities.

What we need is not merely a new artistic current that would reflect these higher ideals, but a complete overthrow of the contemporary cultural order (or, rather, *disorder*), a revolution in the way that modern society functions. The key to restoring enthusiasm among our kinsmen lies in planting seeds of hope, depth, and beauty in every little thing we do. For example, the joy of boundless, romantic love sounds to modern ears more like an idealised emotional state from a fairy tale. As a matter of fact, there is nothing stopping us from reaching a state of near perfection in human relationships. People are scared of perfection to such an extent that they deny the possibility of attaining it. Let us cast aside the fear of failure. Let us stand up against the flooding waves of mediocrity and degeneracy. Let our goodness, excellence, and courage shine brightly with the strength of a thousand suns.

Much wisdom can be found in ancient scriptures and books of the days gone by. J. R. R. Tolkien's works can ignite motivation and hope in our daily struggles. Indeed, the fundamental issues we face today resemble the War of the Ring. Against all odds, the forces of Men, Dwarves, and Elves engage in a conflict with servants of the Red Eye and the White Hand. The situation seems quite hopeless but thanks to the extraordinary heroism of characters like Frodo, Gandalf, and Aragorn, the free peoples of Middle-earth eventually win the war and thrive afterwards. Many of you are likely already aware that Tolkien drew much of his inspiration from the mythologies and epic poems of the classical world. I would recommend everyone to read excerpts from such texts every morning and evening. Instead of vacantly gazing into the hypnotizing abyss of the television screen, let us seek daily advice in the *Bhagavad Gita*, *The Republic*, *Hávamál* or *Enchiridion*. Instead of aimlessly scrolling through our social media feed, let us meditate in silence for a while, in order to reconnect with the greatest possible source of enthusiasm.

Bitterness and pessimism used to be almost exclusively associated with the elderly, who have experienced enough disappointments and horrors in their long lives. But today the lack of enthusiasm affects all age groups. It is prevalent even among the youngest of teenagers! There are multiple reasons for this. For a very long time now we have been lacking both spiritual and political leaders. We have been lacking good and positive role models who could elevate our entire society with their firmness, unwavering courage, and moral uprightness. How can our youngest generation feel hopeful about anything, when the world is ruled by talentless, half-naked pop stars, inauthentic spiritual gurus, and unqualified, corrupt political leaders, who endlessly echo the hollow slogans of peace and equality? How can our children grow into mature and psychologically healthy adults if they are literally nursed by Hollywood and MTV? The poisonous influence of these (and many other) companies on young people's development should not be underestimated. The mainstream media are filled to the brim with anti-traditionalist propaganda. Contemporary film directors' obsession with creating characters of blunt, strong, independent women and passive, effeminate men is one example of how confusion regarding gender roles is planted in the minds of the young. There is much more to be said on the entertainment industry, but it would exceed the confines of this work to discuss those issues in detail.

All things considered, the elites want us to live a life devoid of any meaning other than making money. Their long-term goal is to convince us that we are nothing more than soulless, random pieces of cosmic debris. This is the reason for an excessive promotion of the ideologies of the flesh and the matter. Contrary to what Marxists believe, the material body is only a small and least significant part of the complex, multi-dimensional constitution of man. The literal reduction of a person to flesh and bones is a modern aberration, non-existent in traditional societies. The ancient Scandinavian tradition can serve as a good illustration of the traditional point of view: it distinguishes between *lyke* (physical body), *hamr* (the astral body), *hugr* (mind), and *öðr* (soul). Similar distinctions existed in all ancient Indo-European cultures, with the Vedanta having the most sophisticated and profound explanation of human nature[3]. Furthermore, there was also a doctrine of transmigration of souls (*metempsychosis*), taught widely from Ireland to India. In Europe, Celtic druids and the Pythagoreans were strong adherents of these teachings. The belief in reincarnation was intricately connected with the law of *karma*, which stressed the impact of ethically or unethically motivated actions on the shape of our future lives. Though ancient Greeks and Romans didn't use the term *karma*, their literature (especially Greek tragedy plays such as Aeschylus' *Oresteia*) indicates sophisticated convictions about supra-human justice, guilt, and fate.

Although life in all traditional cultures was not devoid of pain, death, and loss, it provided easily accessible tools and strategies for transforming our existence into something truly joyful and meaningful. The purpose of traditions, customs, and rituals (originating from above, and revealed to mankind by venerable sages) was to remind us of our divine part (*öðr/atman*) and to help us limit our toxic attachment to physical body and false ego – the main sources of misery, greed, lust, envy, and egocentrism. The *coryphaei* of progress have lied to us when they claimed that the death of religion will liberate mankind. The current state of affairs proves that the opposite is true. It is clear that people have never been unhappier than they are now, in this secular and highly materialistic society. In such a world, even complex diseases such as depression are perceived in purely physicalistic[4] terms. What was formerly characterized as a failure to answer positively to

---

3   R. Guénon, *Man and His Becoming According to the Vedanta* (Hillsdale, NY: Sophia Perennis, 2004).

4   Physicalism is a doctrine stating that everything is physical, and that everything in the world can be reduced down to matter and energy.

one of the most important philosophical questions (*what is the meaning of my life?*), coupled with an overwhelming sense of sadness and emptiness, is now *just* a chemical imbalance in the brain! Those who rule the world create artificial living conditions that induce nothing but misery, and then try to alleviate that unhappiness by offering us equally artificial remedies.

We, radical traditionalists, believe that it is our sacred duty to thwart their insidious and baneful attempts at undermining the health and strength of our culture. Henceforth, we declare a metapolitical war against modern superficiality, hopelessness, and degeneracy. Let our brilliant, divine-inspired acts of beauty, honour, and courage break the thick, dark ice of the Kali Yuga. Let the Sun of Tradition slant upon the darkness of the modern world, just like the apricity of the winter sun brings warmth and hope to our slumbering hearts, deeply yearning for springtime.

Aurë entuluva! Day shall come again!

ON COMFORT

Barbarism is the natural state of mankind. Civilization is unnatural. It is a whim of circumstance. And barbarism must always ultimately triumph.
– Robert E. Howard

A Swedish girl called Ida was reading a book at her desk. The mellow light of the lamp filled the room with a tranquil cosiness. The young lady was drinking a cup of coffee flavoured with a pinch of cinnamon and a spoon of honey. She was wearing a red, hand-knitted sweater made of wool. The pleasant warmth of her room contrasted sharply with the relentless downpour outside the window. The rain was pounding upon the roof like a hammer upon a nail. A moment later, Ida looked up from the book and gazed longingly at the water drops running down the window pane. Her cloudless blue eyes reflected a celestial softness and innocence. A strong sense of safety soothed her mind. Although Ida usually tolerated severe weather conditions very well, she was feeling thankful for having a warm and comfortable room to stay in.

***

Had it not been for comfort, our species would not have survived. In the first years of our lives, we are protected and nurtured by motherly love. We share our daily experiences, joys, and worries with family members and friends, whose presence greatly shapes our thoughts and actions. We gather around the hearth to warm ourselves up in front of the flickering flames. We spare no effort to make our bedrooms as cosy as possible, in order to get restful sleep. In every national cuisine, we can find examples of so-called comfort food which is consumed to reduce stress and to enhance our mental well-being. The morning cup of coffee with its refreshing qualities is a crucial part of many people's daily routine. In the summertime, air conditioning removes heat and moisture from inside houses. Umbrellas protect us from autumnal rains. During cold winter evenings, we put on warm sweaters, treat ourselves with hot drinks, and insulate our homes with carpets and curtains.

Thanks to modern technological advancements, we can traverse great distances in cars, trains, and planes. The Internet allows us to communicate with people from all over the world. On-demand services make it possible to enjoy our favourite music and movies in the comfort of our beds whilst eating a delicious pizza delivered right to our door. Provided we have enough money, most of our whimsical desires and wild fantasies can be satisfied in the blink of an eye. Advanced security systems protect our properties against burglars and unwelcome guests. What would have been the reaction of an Iron Age Celtic chieftain if he had been informed that in the 21st century an average citizen is able to live in the lap of luxury? This luxury and material affluence would have been unimaginable even to the wealthiest kings and queens of the past.

One example of how the yearning for an ever-increasing comfort level manifests itself in the modern world is our contemporaries' obsession with cars. Walking is no longer fashionable. Walking is a waste of time, they say. Fewer and fewer children walk or cycle to school, most are driven there by their parents. The sight of faithful Christians going to church *on foot* in order to attend Sunday Mass can no longer be taken for granted. Even a short stroll to the nearby grocery store has been replaced by a *shorter* car ride. In every aspect of human life, we can see that the modern man has accepted to live under the reign of convenience out of his own volition.

But do we really need so much comfort? What are the long-term consequences of living in maximum comfort? Can the complete absence of pain and discomfort make us happier? Growing number of lifestyle diseases (otherwise known as diseases of affluence) proves that we have forgotten about something important in our blind pursuit of materialistic happiness. The lack of exercise, too much stress, an unhealthy diet, and little or no exposure to non-artificial environments lower our natural immunity, thus increasing the risk of obesity, heart disease, cancer, diabetes, and allergies.

***

A great host of vapour ghosts occupied the steep slopes of the mountain, obscuring its naked, slumbering beauty. The loudness of unheard murmurings echoed throughout the glens and hills, altering their halcyon greenery into the uncanny presence of a burial mound.

In the misty greyness of a late October afternoon, amidst heather enshrouded in dew, a dim figure could be seen in the distance. A hooded person trod through bare and quiet, yet sorrowful moorlands. The air was heavy with chill dampness, brought by the northern wind from the Orkney Islands. Although the wayfarer was wrapped up in a thick brat made of deerskin, he was shivering in a patchy drizzle, just like a prematurely buried man, who suddenly awakes from his cataleptic slumber in the middle of a cold winter night. The mysterious wanderer had blue checked trousers, fastened by an intricately decorated belt worn around the waist. The belt supported a sword scabbard. In his hand – a willow staff. So he marched on, in the growing semi-darkness of a dead Caledonian autumn.

**

In Classical Antiquity, daily life was a struggle for survival. The scarcity of food, simpler living conditions, frequent wars, and the lack of sophisticated protection against serious illnesses and severe weather conditions, forced people to step out of their comfort zones. Most of the ancient Indo-European religions and philosophical systems encourage us to perceive discomfort and struggle as ideal opportunities for self-improvement and spiritual growth. In the *Bhagavad Gita*, Lord Krishna says to his devotee Arjuna that those who are deeply attached to *bhog* (gratification) and *aiśhwarya* (luxury), are blind to the divine aspect of life[5]. The Stoic philosophers stress the importance of pursuing voluntary discomfort and the delay of immediate gratification. We can only appreciate the comfort of a warm bed and hot shower after a few weeks spent on strenuous hiking, sleeping in the wilderness, and washing our body in chilly streams and lakes. Likewise, we will never recognize the full worth of drinking water, until we end up on a sun-scorched desert, where the only relief is a misleading mirage of an oasis. However, the key to the gates of wisdom lies neither in a life full of hedonistic pleasures nor in rigorously abstinent asceticism. What we should seek is a sense of balance, and the essence of balance is moderation in detachment. In the following paragraphs, I shall explain how we can find the golden mean between comfort and discomfort.

We learn from Diodorus Siculus, a Greek historian who lived in the 1st century BCE, that ancient Gaulish people slept on animal furs around the hearth, and that they also dined sitting on them. In Ireland, a few centuries after Christ, living conditions in small rural homesteads probably did not differ too much from those in ancient Gaul. After all, in the early medieval tale of Cuchulainn and Ferdia we find a reference to the use of skin coverings as bedclothes: a charioteer asks for skin covering to be put under his head so that he can sleep for a while[6].

It is also interesting to note that Giraldus Cambriensis, writing in the late 12th century, said that his fellow Welshmen had no tables at all at their meals. Sleeping on a mattress is a relatively new phenomenon, and research shows that it isn't necessarily the best surface to rest our bodies on. It is

---

5   *Bhagavad Gita*, 2.44.

6   M. Green, *Animals in Celtic Life and Myth* (London: Routledge, 1992), p. 42.

beyond any question that too much softness (represented by cushions and soft mattresses) makes us weaker. Human beings in industrialized societies have lost a direct and uninterrupted contact with the earth. Sleeping on the floor allows our spine to realign to its natural posture much more easily. It is also said that it prevents back pain and improves blood flow. Considering the evidence, I strongly recommend trying this for yourselves at least for a few nights. Make sure you still insulate your body from the cold, by laying a blanket on the floor. After several such "grounding sessions", you will surely appreciate the luxury of sleeping in a bed. More importantly, however, you will toughen yourself up and gain the ability to be comfortable sleeping anywhere.

The next step is to consider implementing cold showers into your daily routine. We have become used to hot water in our homes to such an extent that we no longer know what it's like to experience real coldness. Cold showers have been proven to have a magical effect on your mood, health, and willpower. The father of medicine, Hippocrates, recommended taking cold baths as a remedy for some illnesses. Both ancient Spartans and Romans often plunged into icy water in order to strengthen their bodies and to recover after battles. In the Victorian era, cold baths were prescribed for pain relief and treatment. What are the benefits of this method? First of all, immersing ourselves in cold water considerably boosts our energy, mood, and alertness – it can work as a great replacement for morning coffee. Secondly, it stimulates weight loss and makes our hair and skin look shinier and healthier. Men who want to increase their testosterone production and fertility should try taking cold showers, as research has demonstrated a strong correlation between them. Last but not least, as soon as we gradually begin reducing our need for hot water, our immune system will compensate by better protecting us against lower temperatures and harsh weather conditions.

However, it is important to state that the complete absence of warm water isn't ideal, either. Cold water is not very effective at removing dirt and bacteria. Those who suffer from heart conditions should consult their doctor before trying cold showers, and I would recommend everyone to begin with contrast showers. Historically, hot baths and sweating baths have been in use since Classical Antiquity. Ancient Greeks and Romans were known for their famous steam baths. The ancient Irish people constructed beehive-shaped buildings known as *toigh-an-alluis* (literally: "the house of perspiration"). Their purpose was remedial of certain diseases such as rheumatism and ague. In Seaton F. Milligan's article from 1889, "The Ancient Irish Hot-Air Bath", we can find the following description of *toigh-an-alluis*:

Sweat houses were common in this part of the country until 50 years ago, and from that time up to twenty years since, they were going out of use. It was heated by fires of turf; when sufficiently hot the coals, ashes, etc. were removed, and some cool thing such as sods, rushes, or stones put in for the persons to stand upon. When men used it, as many as six or eight stripped off and went in, then all openings were closed except what afforded a little ventilation. A person remained outside to attend to these matters. When they could suffer the heat no longer, the flag was removed, and they came out and plunged into a pool of water within a yard or two of the sweat house, where they washed, got well rubbed and put on their clothes. In case of women, they put on a bathing dress whilst using the bath, and generally omitted the plunge or cold bath. People had to be careful not to lean against the walls inside, otherwise they would get burned.[7]

The Roman writer Tacitus reported that ancient Germanic peoples enjoyed having warm water baths in the morning[8]. All the barbaric peoples of Europe had a form of sweat bath or a sauna (e.g. Slavic *banya*), as their healing and restorative properties had been discovered very early.

My main point in this essay is that rather than completely removing comfort from our lives, we should get rid of unnecessary and unwholesome modern luxuries that foster vice. Softness, warmth, and instant gratification of our desires are not good in the long run, and they turn us into lazy and weak creatures, completely dependent on civilization and technological facilities. In order to reach our full potential, we also need to experience discomfort, cold, hunger, and struggle. Trying out the aforementioned cold showers and sleeping on the floor is merely one suggestion, and there are many other ideas worth considering. For example, relying less on cars or on public transportation and choosing (whenever it's possible) to walk or to cycle instead – a much cheaper and healthier alternative. Learning how to endure minor inconveniences, such as an electricity blackout, intense exercise or manual labour, superficial injury, moderate rainfall (why do we have to use an umbrella every time it rains?), or a summer heatwave, will not only help us overcome greater struggles in future, but it will shatter the

---

7   Milligan, Seaton F., *The Ancient Irish Hot: Air Bath.*, The Journal of the Royal Historical and Archaeological Association of Ireland, vol. 9, no. 81, 1889, pp. 268–270.

8   Tacitus, *Germania*, 22.

false illusion that we must preserve our comfort at all costs. Naturally, I have to stress once again that acting without restraint in our quest for daily adversities is obviously not desirable. We must strive for a fine balance between decadent hedonism and voluntary self-torture.

ON HEROISM

He charged before three hundred of the finest,
He cut down both centre and wing,
He excelled in the forefront of the noblest host,
He gave gifts of horses from the herd in winter.
He fed black ravens on the rampart of a fortress
Though he was no Arthur.
Among the powerful ones in battle,
In the front rank, Gwawrddur was a palisade.
– Aneirin, *Y Gododdin*[9]

In J.R.R. Tolkien's *Silmarillion* it is said that after the disastrous battle of Dagor Bragollach, Fingolfin, the high king of the Noldor, filled with wrath and anguish, rode alone to Angband's gates. He blew his horn, banged loudly on the brazen gates, and challenged Morgoth to a duel. The Dark Lord came forth from his underground dwelling, clad in black armour and iron crown, armed with shield and his giant hammer called Grond. He stood before Fingolfin like a lofty tower, throwing a dark shadow of doom over him. But the Elven king feared not, for his silver mail and his blue, crystal-inlaid shield glistened like a brilliant star. Then the fight began. Each time Morgoth tried to crush his opponent with the thundering hammer Grond, Fingolfin dashed away. Seven times Morgoth was wounded with the icy sword Ringil. Eventually, as the elf was becoming increasingly weary, the Dark Lord pinned his left foot upon Fingolfin's neck, killing him. However, the Noldor's last desperate strike hewed Morgoth's foot, leaving his foe with a permanent limp from the injury. Thus ended one of the most heroic yet tragic duels in the history of Arda[10].

***

One reason why Tolkien's books have had such a tremendous impact on our culture and people's imagination, is because they depict a heroic society of warriors, kings and queens, in which there is no place for mediocrity, something so omnipresent in our modern times. In the world of Arda,

---

9   *Y Gododdin* is a medieval Welsh poem consisting of elegies for the men of the Northern Brythonic kingdom of Gododdin, who died fighting the Angles at the disastrous battle of Catraeth. The poem contains one of the earliest possible references to the semi-legendary King Arthur.

10   J.R.R. Tolkien, *The Silmarillion* (London: HarperCollinsPublishers, 1999), pp. 178-179.

honour is almost always a matter of life and death. Solemn oaths are taken, acts of vengeance are executed. Characters created by Tolkien are made of flesh and bone: they feel anger, love, grief, doubt, and joy. Even dark and treacherous entities, like the aforementioned Morgoth, are driven by extreme feelings of pure hatred and bitterness. Especially in the First Age, we find numerous cases of extraordinary heroism. In a dangerous quest to retrieve the Silmaril from Morgoth's iron crown, Beren and Luthien successfully sneaked into Angband and stole the jewel. They managed to return to Doriath, although on their way out they were attacked by a giant wolf called Carcharoth, who bit off Beren's hand containing the Silmaril and swallowed it[11]. In another tale, Glaurung the Dragon wished to assault the woodland realm of Brethil and decided to cross over Cabed-en-Aras, a deep ravine in the river Taeglin. Turin Turambar, after having successfully climbed up the perilous gorge, slew the beast with his own sword Gurthang[12].

In our relatively peaceful modern times, we no longer witness true acts of heroism. Even military conflicts are no longer heroic: contrary to what people think, killing someone with a machine gun bullet (not to mention weapons such as grenades or bombs) is not honourable. In most cases, your enemy does not even get the chance to see whence a fatal gunshot wound came. It is as disgraceful as stabbing someone in the back. Moreover, the wars taking place in the modern world are completely devoid of any transcendental meaning and significance. Empty slogans of nationalism and patriotism cannot conceal the simple truth: people fight for purely materialistic and economic reasons. How did warfare look like in the past? Were ancient conflicts always handled in a noble and respectful way? Isn't war mainly about killing without being killed, by any means necessary?

If we study battle narratives in the Indo-European epic tales, we will be astonished by their heroic and solemn character. Unlike today, many ancient battles (and even minor disputes) were resolved through a series of hand-to-hand duels between individual champions from the opposing sides. For example, the entire Trojan War in the *Iliad* or the Battle of Roncevaux Pass in *The Song of Roland* are depicted as such. The duel (*holmgang* in the Norse tradition) was usually fought in a pre-determined narrow location. Before combat began, it was customary practice for warriors to reveal their identity and lineage. We see a similar pattern in *Silmarillion*, in which Húrin (the father of Túrin Turambar) refused to wear hear his dragon helmet, for he wanted to look at the enemy with his own eyes. Oftentimes, the

11   *Ibid.*, 211-214.

12   *Ibid.*, 264-267.

champions would also hurl intimidating insults at each other. Only then would the battle finally begin.

Historically, the perception of ranged combat varied amongst different ancient Indo-European peoples, but, as a general rule, hand-to-hand combat was always seen as preferable in the upper social strata. The ancient Spartiates (Spartan citizens with full rights) in the Classical period despised archery, perceiving it as a cowardly and womanly skill. Only helots (non-free inhabitants of Sparta), and perhaps mercenaries, were allowed to use bows in the ranks of the Spartan army. It was not until the Second Punic War that the Romans started to incorporate auxiliary units of archers and sling-men into their armies. The former were mostly recruited from the island of Crete, while the latter came from the Balearic Islands. In archaic, semi-legendary Celtic warfare, the sling seemed to be a relatively popular weapon. Lugh slew his giant grandfather Balor with a sling-stone. Cuchulainn was said to have brought down eight swans with a single sling-shot. In the Celtic Iron Age, we have archaeological and literary evidence that slings were used in siege warfare, both for defensive and offensive purposes[13]. Let us not forget about the famous bowman Arjuna from the Vedic epic poem *Mahabharata*. In general, however, slings and bows were weapons of the poor, who may not have been able to afford the spears and shields required for melee combat.

What we have described thus far is just one, profane aspect of classical warfare. What concerns us the most is the sacred, transcendental dimension inherently present in heroism. From this perspective, war is not just a favourable occasion for displaying martial prowess, knightly behaviour and risking one's health or life for the sake of earthly community, tribe, king, or (as is especially true of the modern world) ideals of patriotism, nationalism, and democracy. For the man of Tradition, this exoteric form of warfare was intricately linked with a far greater, inner conflict – between what attaches him to the earth (instincts, emotions, desires) and what goes beyond this attachment. In other words, the battlefield was an outer plane through which an act of inner self-mastery, aimed at connecting to the divine in man, could have been realized.

For the sake of clarity, let us now analyse some practical examples of this twofold doctrine that we have just expounded. According to the reports of the classical authors, Gaulish druids taught the doctrine of the immortality of the human soul and of its capacity to reincarnate into

---

13   B. Cunliffe, *Iron Age Communities in Britain* (Abingdon: Routledge, 2005), p. 534.

another form after bodily death. Inspired by this belief, many Gaulish warriors discarded the fear of death in battle. The Greek historian Polybius mentions a group of Celtic mercenaries called *Gaesatae*, who reportedly went into battle naked[14]. From an earthly point of view, the popular explanation is that ritual nudity was meant to unnerve their enemies and allow greater mobility. However, the esoteric dimension of this custom implies a disregard for earthly attachments (such as the care for one's body) and yearning for transcendence, strengthened by the above-mentioned doctrine of reincarnation. Appian of Alexandria, writing in the 2nd century CE, remarks that the Teutonic peoples had no fear of death because they believed in rebirth[15]. In the later Old Norse tradition, there was a belief that the bravest warriors fallen on the battlefield were taken by Valkyries ("the choosers of the slain") to Valhalla ("the hall of the slain"), where they joined the celestial host of Odin. Valkyries symbolize the transcendental part of a warrior's constitution, triumphant over lower material senses and instincts. All things considered, warfare in the world of Tradition gave the man of action a chance for inner, spiritual realization. This sacred dimension is completely absent from the modern world, which unfortunately acknowledges only the profane, naturalistic aspect of warfare[16].

The invention of the machine gun was the final nail in the coffin for heroic warfare. The absence of real heroism in our modern society necessitated the invention of artificial forms of hardships and adversities. A hero of today can be a popular football player, a successful celebrity or even a charity benefactor. Our yearning for chivalry and noble deeds has found an outlet in the realm of art and entertainment: fantasy novels (Tolkien's previously mentioned works are the best example), popular movies, historical re-enactment, role-playing games or epic music genres – they originate from our desperate efforts to fill the spiritual void of modernity. So long as society is based upon the ideas of radical egalitarianism, however, our attempts are largely futile. Those ideas have become predominant primarily because of Abrahamic religions. With its poisonous ideas of tolerance, equality, self-abnegation, and submissiveness, Christianity has corrupted our pagan understanding of what a virtuous life should look like. Even though most Europeans no longer practise Christianity, our secular governments, universities and schools (influenced

---

14   Polybius, *Histories*, 2.28.

15   Appian, *Celtica*, 1.3.9.

16   For a more detailed discussion of this subject see: J. Evola, *Metaphysics of War* (Arktos, 2011).

by Cultural Marxism and postmodernism) try to teach people to act and behave in an unnatural way.

It is my firm opinion that we need to fundamentally redefine the definition of heroism. There is no return to the heroic warfare of the Classical Antiquity. Joining the modern military is not a good solution, either – wars in the 21st century serve the interests of bankers and politicians. These are *not* our wars. But heroism is not only about physical combat. It is also a mental struggle to swim against the current, to be a true individualist who is not concerned with the opinion of crowds. A hero is a person who revolts against the modern world by rejecting and disassociating from its trends, fashions, and institutions. He chooses a simple, virtuous, and traditional life in the countryside over the hustle and bustle of big cities, endless money-making, material affluence and *artificial paradises*[17]. A hero is someone who has a sharp, tough, and Stoic mindset. He perceives discomfort, misfortune, and adversities as perfect opportunities for self-improvement. He is never afraid to take *calculated* risks. He fully recognizes the crucial importance of physical fitness in our daily life. His willingness to become stronger and more agile has a genuine and profound motivation – he works out not to mask his vain insecurities, but to honour and cultivate a divine part of his soul. A strong body reflects spiritual might. He treats women with utmost respect and gentleness. For him, honour is always a matter of life and death – just like in Middle-Earth.

Can women also display a heroic attitude of mind? Absolutely, although there are some essential differences between feminine heroism and masculine heroism. For women, giving birth to children and homeschooling them is the greatest act of revolt against the modern world. A heroine is a woman who fully recognizes the hidden traps and evils of modern feminism and embraces her innate femininity instead. Acting against the unnatural expectations of modern society, she seeks to fulfil her true potential through the path of marriage and motherhood. By giving herself to one and only one man, she plants a seed of divine inspiration in his soul. She nourishes him (and their children) with her unconditional love, warmth and understanding. In the history of mankind, many great ambitions and plans could not have come to fruition without the spiritual support of a woman.

---

17   *Artificial Paradises* is a book by French poet Charles Baudelaire, first published in 1860, about the effects of the intake of opium and hashish.

ON TALENTS

Conformity to one's caste was considered by traditional humanity as the first and main duty of an individual.
– Julius Evola[18]

Naturally, the general principles I have discussed in the previous essay can be slightly adjusted in accordance with individual differences in men and women. When we think of a virtuous life and heroism, we need to take into consideration one's temperament, physical and mental constitution, and life history. Not every man is destined to become a warrior and a champion of body and it is perfectly normal that some men may choose a path of a scholar or a craftsman. These paths are no less honourable if they are followed in consonance with the natural law (*dharma*), which manifests itself differently in every individual (*svadharma*). Not every woman is destined to have children (for various, often complicated reasons, such as infertility or severe emotional traumas), and it is perfectly normal that some women may decide to serve the community through alternative means. There is a worrying tendency among men in traditionalist circles to frown upon unmarried and childless women. It is beyond any shadow of doubt that deciding to become a mother is a very noble act, but it is also men's duty to treat women with respect, regardless of their personal choices and limitations.

Such personal tendencies and predispositions are sorted out by the ancient Indo-European system of self-analysis known as *varna*. In the Vedic tradition, there were four main categories of psycho-physiological constitution that indicate one's preferred vocation: *brahmana* (those who are naturally inclined toward intellectual, spiritual, and artistic occupations), *kshattriya* (those who have a natural predisposition toward political, administrative or military tasks), *vaishya* (those who have a special aptitude for tradesmanship and agriculture), and *shudra* (those who realize their true potential through manual labour). They were frequently likened to the different parts of the body, each section responsible for its own, specific role in supporting the entire organism. These categories existed in equivalent or very similar forms in other Indo-European societies. For example, in pre-Islamic Iran, there were four main socio-psychological classes: *asravan* (priests), *arteshtaran* (warriors), v*astriya-fshuyant* (merchants), and *vastryoshan* (commoners). The tribal communities of the ancient Celts were characterized by a threefold division into the following

---

18   J. Evola, *Revolt Against the Modern World* (Rochester, VT: Inner Traditions, 1995), p. 89.

classes: druids (the intelligentsia – priests, judges, teachers, physicians, historians, poets...), nobles and warriors (likened by Julius Caesar to the Roman *equites*), and the commoners.

Our contemporaries who believe in the false, modern notion of egalitarianism may not know that hierarchy is in fact something completely natural. Enamoured with the democratic tendencies of the present age and the delusional pipe-dreams of liberalism, they tend to frown upon authoritative, hierarchical social orders of the past which, according to them, severely curtailed individual freedom. At the same time, they seem not to have any serious objections against being slaves to global consumerism and living under the totalitarian reign of mass media. In every traditional culture, individuals with higher intellectual, moral, and charismatic capabilities were given tasks vital to the survival of the society. Conversely, those without such skills were satisfied with pursuing vocations of craftsmen, merchants or labourers. There was no shame in belonging to one of the lower strata, as long as one's caste-determined duties were duly performed, and vertical transgression did not occur (with very few permissible exceptions in times of distress). The notion of *varna* was not based on oppression and intolerance, but rather on the promotion of harmony and efficient cooperation between differing human natures that constituted society as a whole. It is only through rational discrimination (understood here as the act of noting and perceiving differences) and strict exclusivity (unique restrictions and rights for each group) that we can achieve common prosperity and happiness.

In the following paragraphs, we are going to discuss how living a virtuous life in accordance with *dharma* manifested itself differently in each of the four major categories. Note that this is just a simplified overview meant to provide a general illustration of how social structure looked like in the Vedic age. Those of you interested in pursuing this subject in further detail should refer to Vedic scriptures[19] that thoroughly explain the origin and the social role of each *varna*, as well as the significance of purification and expiation rites in each group. I have chosen to describe this particular social stratification system not because I am prejudiced in favour of Orientalism (as some people might wrongly assume), but simply because the common Indo-European tradition in question is best preserved in the scriptures of Vedic India. Therefore, I find it perfectly reasonable that those Europeans who wish to rediscover their pre-Abrahamic roots should look for guidance in the traditions of the East.

Brahmanas are naturally predisposed toward vocational activities of

---

19   Such as *Manusmriti* (*The Laws of Manu*).

scholarship, writing, teaching, and counselling. In their daily conduct, they should exhibit character traits such as patience, humility, calmness, self-control, and truthfulness. Unless a *brahmana* finds himself in exceptional circumstances (e.g. self-defence in war and other times of distress), he is prescribed to avoid using violence and causing harm to other living beings (*ahimsa*). Despite being mainly concerned with intellectual and spiritual matters, he should not forget about taking care of his physical health as well. Light to moderate exercise, cleanliness, and proper diet are highly recommended for the sake of providing a stable physical foundation to his intellectual labour. The acquisition of wealth by him should not be used for the purposes of pleasure, but for the sake of subsistence. It is important to remember that neither spirituality nor scholarship are a business and they should never be treated as such.

Kshatriyas excel in tasks that require administrative, political, and military skills. Their primary duty is to protect the social-cosmic *dharmic* order: defend the nation's interests, guard the weak against the strong, and make sure that the law is not transgressed. In their daily conduct, they should exhibit character traits such as courage, charisma, gravity, confidence, decisiveness, firmness, prudence, and equitability. *Kshatriyas* should spend the greater part of their time on building up physical strength, stamina, and martial prowess. They need to be alert to the potential pitfalls of becoming overly arrogant and recklessly bold, especially when they deal with matters of national importance. Similarly, they need to make themselves immune to corruption, drunkenness, and an inordinate attachment to women, for these vices becloud their wisdom and vitality. Those who defy *dharma* should fear them as dangerous and aggressive foes, but an excess of brutality and unnecessary violence deserves strong condemnation, especially when directed towards women, children, and the elderly. Last but not least, let their innate aptitude for formulating political strategy and taking firm action be combined with the invaluable advice of the wise and the learned men (*brahmanas*). A state built upon the communion between action and contemplation shall never perish.

Vaishyas are focused on agriculture, cattle-tending, trade, money-lending, and business. In their daily conduct, they should exhibit character traits such as honesty, industriousness, exuberance, diligence, politeness, and tactfulness. Merchants should always maintain the high quality of products they sell, set fair and reasonable prices, avoid charging people for services that require minimal or no cost or effort and make sure they do not use emotional manipulation in advertisement. When it comes to money-lending, usury should be strictly prohibited, as well as any other dishonest, greed-driven means of generating income. Agriculturists should put their effort and time into making the best use of the outcomes of their work. They should avoid ruthlessly exploiting soil (e.g. causing soil erosion due to improper extractive practices) and livestock (e.g. cruelty to animals) out of covetousness.

Shudras realize their true potential through manual labour, those are e.g. carpenters, metalworkers, artisans, construction workers, butchers, fishermen or barbers. In their daily conduct, they should exhibit character traits such as loyalty, precision, earnestness, modesty, and simplicity. *Shudras* have a materialistic, down-to-earth nature that precludes them from understanding the intricacies of the religious scriptures and pursuing intellectual vocations. However, it doesn't mean that they cannot contribute to the overall well-being of society. Quite the contrary: through their sincere devotion to serving others and following simple, ethical rules prescribed for their *varna* (as well as following the example of virtuous men), they provide a solid foundation for the efficient functioning of the entire society.

The recognition of the superiority of pontifical and regal powers, and their close connection with the transcendent realm of life (sanctioned by initiatory rites), was once widespread and unshakeable. It was only with the advent of democratic ideas and the growing secularization of society that the acceptance of higher authority began to crumble, and the lower social classes usurped the throne and the sceptre, reducing their profound metaphysical significance to a mere sign of political and temporal power. Finally, the recent blights of egalitarianism and globalisation brought nothing but a further blow to the hierarchical systems rooted in transcendence.

In the present Age of Kali, everything that was cherished by the man of Tradition is either already gone or in a state of complete dissolution and decline. Owing to those processes, people nowadays are totally confused when it comes to the recognition of their innate calling and the choice of occupation they are predisposed to. Captivated by the superficial glamour of the so-called American Dream, which is based upon the false notion that "all men are created equal", they gravitate towards the most socially prestigious and lucrative careers, without taking into account whether those desirable paths are compatible with their true nature. What matters to our contemporaries is no longer descent and hereditary character, but mere effort and merit. It is, of course, beyond any question that the latter are essential factors in determining one's worth as a human being. However, due to unrestricted social mobility, even a shoemaker can become an influential politician, as long as he has the minimal intellect required to deceive people (because this is what most modern politicians sadly do). It is commonly believed that standardized examination tests at school measure a person's competence for a career of his or her choice. That is to a certain degree true, but what they really evaluate is the ability to memorize given information in order to later reproduce it during these examinations. After repeated exposure to such tasks, a student's academic performance improves. Interestingly enough, this measurement very often does not correspond with a learner's actual understanding of the subject. As is frequently the case with many other overly-quantitative inventions of the modern age, examination tests do not take into consideration one's inner constitution, interests, moral character, and possible ways in which he or she could contribute to the betterment of their entire community. Thus, we can conclude that the public education system in its current state is not an authoritative method of evaluing one's merit. Fortunately, there are still good (though not ideal) alternatives to sending your children to public school. Thoughtful parents should consider homeschooling or Waldorf education, as these are some of the few options that put a strong emphasis on children's holistic development (evaluated mainly through qualitative description), rather than just teaching them how to solve standardized tests.

The whole atmosphere of an incessant rat race causes chronic anxiety about one's social status. People in the Kali Yuga are obsessed with career advancement and meaningless money-making *ad infinitum*. They never bother to look inward, to determine whether their current occupation is compatible with the *varna* they belong to. Always in frenetic motion, deaf and blind to anything that escapes the notion of their senses, never satisfied with what they have – such is the nature of modern men. Unfortunately, the world has devolved so far from the ideals of the Golden Age that it is virtually impossible to recreate the sacred hierarchical order that we have just described in the previous paragraphs. It's hard to know what to do in such unfavourable circumstances. In spite of all the gloom and degeneracy that surrounds us, there are still noble-hearted individuals who do not fall for the siren-like calls of modernity and who refuse to be contaminated by the noxious doctrines of progress. On the outside, they appear to look like everyone else, but inwardly they carry the inextinguishable flame of Tradition that allows them to successfully act in the material world, while simultaneously being detached from it. Such an enlightened individual (a *karma yogi*[20]) is focused solely on performing his duty (determined by his *varna*) in accordance with *dharma*. Fixed in transcendence, he is equally indifferent to success and failure or reward and punishment. Amidst the

---

20   The principles of *karma yoga* are expounded in Chapter Three of the *Bhagavad Gita*.

greatest external turmoil, he remains calm and resistant to urges (such as desire or anger) that might compromise his duty. Although he operates within the imperfect material world (thus he is subject to its laws), his action is purified because it has been committed with spiritual purpose at its core (e.g. a policeman who is frequently forced to use violence while fighting crime). In my opinion, this is the most reasonable way in which an intelligent and sane individual (who has little in common with the mindless crowds of the present age) can still lead a fulfilling and joyful life.

ON PARENTHOOD

A nation is created by families, a religion, a tradition: it is made up out of the hearts of mothers, the wisdom of fathers, the joy and the exuberance of children.
– Kaiser Wilhelm II

In the present age of Kali, being born in a large, close-knit and supportive family is no longer the norm, but rather the exception. There are many reasons for the dissolution of extended family networks and the growing decline of the nuclear family model. It is outside of the scope of this work to discuss them in detail. Instead, we will focus solely on determining what are the most sensible solutions for this crisis of the traditional family. Given the current state of the world, we can not expect every person to desire the pursuit of typical family life. On the other hand, we must be wary not to fall into the trap of selfish individualism and complete neglect of supra-individual duties. Therefore, I propose two possible paths one can consider embarking upon.

First of all, we have persons who are naturally family-oriented. They were either raised in non-dysfunctional families that provided positive parental role models or they were born in less favourable circumstances but overcame them early on in their lives because they had supportive grandparents or aunts and uncles. Family-oriented individuals should ideally be free from the adverse consequences of psychological traumas, in the sense that it is essential to be emotionally stable before becoming a parent. Such persons are advised to have as many children as they can afford to have. Mothers are encouraged to stay at home and educate their offspring, while fathers should prioritize providing for the family. Large families sharing a similar, traditional outlook on life should settle down not very far from each other, so that their children are provided with a chance for meaningful socialization.

Then we have persons who are definitely not family-oriented. They were most likely raised in dysfunctional families that significantly undermined their ability to become loving and supportive parents. Lacking parental love (and not having any substitute of it), they were more likely to experience all sorts of psychological problems and traumas in the later course of their lives. Such persons are often loners and prefer solitary activities. Although they shouldn't completely reject the idea of having children (they may want to have just one child), they must humbly realize their limitations in this particular matter. Contrary to what some traditionalists say, it is not a shame to place a lower priority on family if one lacks skills and predispositions to become a good parent. One can still lead a meaningful and socially positive life without having many children. Such individuals should prioritize finding a practical, altruistic way in which they can contribute to the overall betterment of their folk. This is not to be equated with mindless money-making and career advancement – the loftiest ideals of Kali Yuga. What is meant here is that those who are not family-oriented are advised to pursue productive activities such as: mastering a traditional craft, preserving old traditions and customs, working on an organic farm, creating divine-inspired art, becoming a teacher or a counsellor, etc. Other than that, such persons may want to consider befriending a large, like-minded family. By doing so, they can not only become supportive friends to the parents in this family, but also act as mentors (*guru*) to the children (without taking up typical parental responsibilities), assisting in what was traditionally known as second, spiritual birth. Their role must not be underestimated.

It is important to remember that these two paths are not mutually exclusive. They merely indicate priorities, which vary between individuals. What works for one person may not work for someone else. In the age of feminism and free love, in which people are deliberately discouraged from embracing traditional gender roles, it is becoming increasingly difficult to learn the art of parenthood. We must coldly recognize the gravity of the situation and formulate a realistic strategy compatible with our inner constitution.

ON MINIMALISM

Our very way of life breeds unhappiness. We have an active and turbulent culture in which there is little peace or contentment. We have disturbed the organ roots of life, which are good food, water, air, and a happy family life. We live in an artificial world dominated by an urban landscape and mass media, in which there is little to nourish the soul.
– David Frawley[21]

More and more individuals are becoming aware of the fact that living under the reign of Quantity has proven detrimental to our psychological and emotional well-being. The ceaseless and frenetic accumulation of material goods has only cluttered our hearts and homes with gloom and misery. A countercultural minimalism movement has arisen in response to these materialistic tendencies. Tens of thousands of people have embarked on a quest to simplify their hectic lives. There are undeniable benefits to leading a minimalist lifestyle, for it shifts our attention away from mindless consumerism and toxic attachment to material possessions. Nonetheless, just like almost every other modern trend, the idea of minimalism has unfortunately been commercialized. This seemingly noble, anti-consumerist lifestyle has gradually turned into yet another sellable fashion.

It is high time to redefine the concept of minimalism. In my view, it has to be grounded in authentic spiritual tradition, thus transcending the limitations of matter. One reason why minimalism has failed as a countercultural movement is because it has never explicitly prioritized spirituality over matter. It has been primarily associated with decluttering one's living space and establishing some healthy mental habits, but not much beyond that. It is true that many followers of minimalism have recommended meditating on a daily basis – a secularized form of this ancient spiritual practice focuses on mindful breathing and repetitive affirmations. It cannot be denied that these habits (separated from their former religious aspects) can still contribute to the overall betterment of human health[22]. However, as long as minimalism has its theoretical foundations built upon secular life, it cannot reach its full potential and remains but a faint shadow of the ancient, venerable traditions, which were designed to help man achieve enlightenment and strengthen his connection with the divine. We have had enough parasitical New Age businessmen leeching off people's misery – it is high time to return to the very roots of

---

21   D. Frawley, *Ayurveda and the Mind* (Twin Lakes, WI: Lotus Press, 2007).

22   More on this in my essay on concentration.

authenticity.

As explained in my essay on enthusiasm, we are much more than just physical bodies. The most important element of our multifaceted constitution is the eternal, transcendental self (*öðr/atman*) of the divine essence. However, in the hustle and bustle of our daily lives, the siren-like calls of the false, temporal ego (*ahamkara*) tempt us to turn away from that radiant source of perfection and bliss, so we voluntarily incarcerate ourselves in the prison of worldly pleasures and materialistic goals. When we embody the positive attributes of righteousness, humility, diligence, and honour, the bonds of our false egos loosen. Conversely, acting with arrogance, greed, malice, and envy prolongs our captivity. The goal of spiritual practice is to completely lift the veils of illusory darkness that conceal from us that innermost, everlasting lightness. Contrary to what some people might think, such liberation does not imply the renunciation of the material world. In my opinion, a healthy attitude to spirituality should also include taking care of our bodies and material needs. Prosperity and affluence should not be frowned upon, as long as they are perceived as temporal (thus imperfect and destructible), intermediary tools which we use to strengthen our connection with the divine order.

A minimalist lifestyle firmly grounded in spirituality is fundamentally different from its secular counterpart. Those who sincerely follow the path of *dharma* are motivated to replicate the bygone Golden Age in every one of their thoughts, words, and actions. They understand that true, long-term happiness can only be found within, not externally. Their yearning for simplicity does not originate from feelings of bitter resentment toward the material world. In fact, some of them may even have successful careers in the secular world. However, they are not fooled by the deceitful glamour of material goods and remain unfaltering in their preference for goods of the higher, spiritual kind. Systematically cultivating such a profound attitude should be the goal of every conscious minimalist.

What is the very first thing we should take into consideration when starting a minimalist lifestyle? Let us look at material possessions in our household. From the spiritual perspective, they can be divided into four main categories. First of all, we have items that serve the function of material vessels for spiritual qualities. Those are philosophical books (e.g. Plato, Julius Evola), ancient religious scriptures (e.g. *The Upanishads*), works of visual art saturated with profound metaphysical significance (e.g. Nicholas Roerich[23], Sandro Botticelli), audio recordings of beautiful music that enhances the best qualities in us (e.g. Hindustani classical music, *raga*),

---

23   Nicholas Roerich (1874 – 1947) was a Russian painter, philosopher, and

devotional images and idols (depicting the pre-Abrahamic, Indo-European pantheon), religious symbols (e.g. Mjölnir) and so forth. Such objects are meant to contribute to our overall spiritual well-being. When we dedicate our attention to them, we are in return nourished by their timeless, inspirational wisdom or beauty. Even though they are made of imperfect and destructible matter, they must be treated with due respect, because of the positive qualities they bestow upon us indirectly. We should never regret spending money on objects from this category, as they serve the function of a window to transcendence.

The second group comprises of objects that usually bring neither benefit nor harm to our spiritual life, but they are to a certain extent necessary for our mental, intellectual survival. Those are primarily non-fiction books (which give us an opportunity to master many fields of knowledge) fiction novels, movies, and games (which stimulate our intellect and provide us with entertainment). I would also be inclined to add electronic devices (computers, mobile phones etc.) to this category because they allow us to communicate with people from all over the world (thus fulfilling our psychological need to socialize). Moreover, when used in a reasonable manner, they are an invaluable source of information and knowledge. However, we have to remember that those devices should not be used for boosting our false ego (e.g. instant gratification and obsessive self-aggrandizing tendencies on social media). Similarly, watching movies or playing games for the sake of mere escapism (especially when it leads to neglecting important duties) has to be avoided whenever possible.

The third category consists of objects that usually bring neither benefit nor harm to our spiritual life, but are more or less necessary for our physical survival. These include clothes (which shelter our bodies from unfavourable weather conditions), food and drinks (which provide our bodies nourishment), household appliances (e.g. washing machine, stove, clothes iron), furniture (which facilitate basic human activities such as sitting, sleeping, and storing items). All these things should be used for practical purposes and not much beyond that. For example, we need clothes to cover our bodies and to feel relatively comfortable in company of others, but buying fancy, fashionable garments feeds nothing but our false ego. Similarly, we should strive for functional simplicity when arranging our living space. An excess of material luxury has to be avoided and replaced with a rich profusion of goods of the higher, spiritual kind.

Last but not least, there are items which explicitly hinder our spiritual development and very frequently harm our physical health as well.

---

archaeologist known for his majestic depictions of the Himalayas.

Examples include: drugs and alcoholic beverages (which becloud our reason), junk food (which weakens our physical health) pornography (which negatively warps our perception of sexuality and significantly decreases male virility), ugly modern art (which perverts our sense of aesthetics), and violent movies and games (which potentially trigger unnecessary aggression). I think that this category is pretty much self-explanatory.

There is still one other aspect that needs to be discussed. In the ancient Vedic tradition, we can find a very interesting concept of the three *gunas* – psychological modes characteristic to the matter (*prakriti*). These qualities are inherently present in everything and everyone, but in varying proportions. *Sattva* is the mode of goodness, harmony, peace, tranquillity, purity, knowledge, and truth. *Rajas* is the mode of passion, activity, excitement, energy, motion, and change. *Tamas* is the mode of imbalance, chaos, darkness, apathy, inertia, and dullness. The three *gunas* can be easily understood if we analyse how they manifest in one's daily life. When we drink a morning cup of coffee in order to boost our energy, when we exercise while listening to martial industrial music, when we are busy accomplishing our daily to-do list – then we are acting in the mode of *rajas*. When we are watching the morning news with an anxious and irritated look on our face, when we shout at someone who made us angry, when we are buying an expensive car because of our greed – then we are also acting in the mode of *rajas*. The quality of *tamas* is related to rest, relaxation, and sleep, which are all good in moderation. An excess of *tamas* occurs when we are lazy, when we procrastinate too much, when we consume alcohol and drugs that becloud our mind or when we engage in binge-watching TV series with a mindless, passive attitude. As we can see, neither of these two modes is inherently good or bad – everything depends on the context. Even the most virtuous of us need a certain amount of *rajas* and *tamas* in order to successfully operate within the confines of the material world. One of many goals of spiritual practice is to cultivate the third quality – *sattva*. When we eat healthy, fresh and nutritious food, when we exhibit positive character traits such as goodness, kindness, tolerance, wisdom, self-control, and calmness, when our thoughts are clear as the azure midsummer sky, when our motives are pure as the perpetual snow on alpine peaks – then we are leading a *sattvic* lifestyle.

Understanding the incessant interplay of the three *gunas* in the material world is certainly helpful if we wish to avoid blindly following negative consumerist trends. For example, a person who is predominantly *rajasic* (thus driven by greed and selfishness, living under the illusory spell of matter) can become obsessed with frenetic money-making because he or she wants to buy new cars and gadgets all the time. Very often we observe that when businessmen or popular celebrities are not busy rushing after gold, they sink even lower, to the mode of *tamas*. Bewildered by the superficial glamour of the sensual pleasures, they participate in mind-numbing consumption and intoxicate themselves, as if they were animals. On the other hand, people who are predominantly *sattvic* are capable of seeing the world as it is. Even when they are walking among the richest of the world, they remain sober in judgement, calm in action, and inwardly detached from the hustle and bustle that surrounds them. Rarely do they stray from their path of virtue. And if they do – they feel remorse and immediately realize their mistake. That cannot be said about those who are perpetually imprisoned in the throes of manic passion or dark ignorance.

The concept of the three *gunas* can also be applied to our environment. For this reason, those individuals who have very little in common with the modern world should consider moving to the countryside because leading a *sattvic* lifestyle is much easier there. Although rapid urbanization is progressively wiping out the pristine beauty and tranquillity of rural regions, it is still possible to find the ideal conditions for making spiritual progress and reinforcing the best tendencies and qualities within us there. This topic is thoroughly explained in my essays about hiking and forest walking. In many European countries, we can find remains of ancient menhirs, stone circles, temples, and sacred groves – these places of worship are saturated with *sattvic* energy. Visiting them is a source of spiritual rejuvenation. Conversely, in the congested city streets and among the gleaming skyscrapers one can find an abundance of *rajas*. An unhealthy spirit of restlessness and competitiveness permeates the minds of human ants crawling through these concrete anthills. Only those who are bewitched by the illusion of attaining happiness through the satiation of endless materialistic cravings may thrive in such artificial urban paradises. Finally, *tamasic* environments include slums, prisons, bars, pubs, cemeteries, and rock or metal concert venues. Because of the high risk of being contaminated by the negativity present there, we should avoid having anything to do with such places.

It might be a bold statement, but I believe that many problems of the modern world (including irrational consumerism and excessive attachment to materialistic luxuries) could be solved if people were educated about the importance of incorporating a *sattvic* mindset and behaviour into their daily lives. A minimalist lifestyle built upon such a profound spiritual foundation is a powerful tool that enables us to maintain balance in everything we do.

ON SOCIOPATHY

Every evil in the bud is easily crushed: as it grows older, it becomes stronger.
– Cicero[24]

Social life in the Kali Yuga is almost completely devoid of empathy. Most human relationships are based on selfish interests, cold calculation, deception, and callous exploitation of each other at all costs. The regression of morality has gone so far that even Machiavellianism and narcissism are now socially acceptable traits. Sociopathy is spreading like a virus. In order to perceive these signs of decline in the clearest and the most vivid form, one need only to take a short peek at social media. I believe that owing to the opportunity for users to remain more or less anonymous and safe in cyberspace, the Internet facilitates irresponsibility and all kinds of traditionally unethical behaviours and attitudes. As has already been said in the essay on progress, the short-sighted obsession of the modern man with unrestricted technological advancement completely disregards the long-term consequences of embracing the latest novelties. In the following paragraphs, I am going to discuss some aspects of sociopathy which I consider one of the gravest dangers of our times. What is more, I shall give practical advice on how to combat sociopaths in the least unethical, yet still effective, way. At the end of the essay, I shall elaborate on the importance of developing our emotional awareness.

Every person is born with the capacity to strengthen within him or her the best, divine qualities and attitudes. Our eternal self is already perfect, but due to the multiple layers of illusion that becloud its presence from our sight, we choose to worship the false ego and the lower qualities of matter (*rajas* and *tamas*). The further we drift from *dharma*, the closer we get to sociopathy, which is surprisingly common in our times. Sociopaths are manipulative individuals who perceive their victims as merely targets and opportunities, not as real human beings with unique personalities and goals. They are incapable of maintaining long-term friendships and very often struggle with romantic relationships. If they ever express positive emotions such as kindness, warmth, and compassion, do not let yourself be fooled by appearances, for they do it just for show. In fact, they have ulterior motives, intentionally concealed behind the veil of superficial charm (sometimes coupled with a sense of humour). Sociopaths are not concerned about the negative impact of their ruthless actions on others. They are experts at pathological lying, gossiping behind people's backs, gaslighting and

---

24   Cicero, *Philippicæ*, v. 11.

humiliating their victims. Yet, being extremely narcissistic, they are easily offended and become enraged when criticized. Sociopaths frequently suffer from delusions of grandeur, and in their arrogance they believe that they are entitled to special treatment.

Interestingly enough, many sociopaths seem to have an interest in gaining influential leadership positions in politics, business and management. They easily earn public trust through their superficial charm and manipulation skills. Once their top position is established and secured, sociopaths will stop at nothing to achieve their selfish ends. They will use every possible immoral means (such as lying, slander, stalking, threats, sabotage, blackmail, etc.) to exercise control over their subjects. It should come as no surprise to us that many powerful political leaders in history were in fact sociopaths (or worse – psychopaths). Examples include: Joseph Stalin, Adolf Hitler, Mao Zedong, Nicolae Ceausescu, Pol Pot, Tamerlane, Elizabeth Bathory, and Caligula. In the age of democracy, sociopathy among the ruling class has become subtler and less visible to the naked eye. How many times have we witnessed our leaders lying, making false promises, and placing blame on their political adversaries in order to evade responsibility? How is it possible that politicians are so desensitized to their own immoral behaviour? How can they constantly deceive entire populations without showing any signs of guilt and remorse?

In the Bhagavad Gita, Lord Krishna distinguishes between two kinds of qualities that characterize human beings: divine (*daivah*) and demoniac (*asurah*)[25]. Our earthly life is like a perpetual battle between these two forces. Our thoughts, intentions, and actions determine which quality is dominant in us at any given moment. The demoniac mind is darkened by ignorance, lust, vanity, and arrogance. Because such people hate themselves and the world around them (misanthropy), their destructive actions bring nothing but chaos, conflict, and dissolution. Indifferent to spirituality and ethics, they do not understand virtues such as mercy, kindness or politeness. As the Kali Yuga advances, demoniac qualities become more and more prevalent in mankind's moral constitution. Conversely, the divine mind shines with goodness, truthfulness, patience, and self-control, just like the sun in a cloudless sky penetrates all corners of the earth with its brilliant warmth. Preferring to hide in the shade of deception and devilry, demoniac persons hate the light, hence their vicious attacks aimed at perverting or destroying anything that blinds their wicked eyes. Such is the inner constitution of sociopaths.

The truth of the matter is that they only appear powerful and bold as

---

25   *Bhagavad Gita*, 16.

long as they are terrorizing others. As soon as they begin to lose their grip, they may exhibit signs of boiling rage and frantic efforts to reassert control. When defeated, sociopaths are exposed as weak, cowardly, and insecure individuals, who feel confident only when they sustain themselves on other people's misery like parasites. Understanding that they are not invincible is crucial if we want to make progress in our dealings with them. When interacting with sociopaths, avoid expressing your real emotions, particularly when you feel anger. Remain cool and unwavering in your assertiveness. Sociopaths prey on vulnerability and gullibility. Conceal or address your weaknesses before they take advantage of them. Do not naively believe that these people can be changed – even if they can, it's not worth the trouble. Such people are not interested in having a reasonable discussion, they won't even listen to your arguments. Thus, your most important duty is not to fight with them, but to protect yourself from damage they may cause to you. The best way to defeat sociopaths is to set clear boundaries and then cut them out of your life. If possible, end communicating with them "cold turkey"; do not provide them with any justification or explanation for your decision. It would be as fruitless as trying to explain Hegel's *Phenomenology of Spirit* to a dog. Just say no and walk away. Stay firm in your resolution not to let them get close to you again.

In order to strengthen our internal resistance against demoniac persons, we should strive to raise our emotional awareness (which is sometimes vaguely called "emotional intelligence"). First and foremost, we need to learn how to be assertive. Contrary to what many good-hearted but naive persons think, not everyone has noble intentions. In particular, women – who are on average more trustful and empathetic than men – need to realize this. When we are surrounded by people who do not wish us well, the only reasonable course of action is to shut the gates. In my opinion, misguided empathy towards strangers is one of the major reasons why entire populations are so easily deceived by politicians (who are not protectors of democracy, but treacherous snakes in suits). We need to learn that not everyone deserves to be treated with kindness. In the modern world there is a growing tendency to justify crimes and other behavioural problems by claiming that the wrongdoer was raised in an abusive environment and had a traumatic childhood. There is no doubt that those factors can help us understand why someone is acting in an ethically erratic way, but they should never serve as a convenient excuse for wrongful conduct.

Secondly, we need to learn how to accurately identify and describe emotional states. This useful skill not only makes it easier to handle negative emotions, but also helps us understand each other. If someone states that they were feeling "bad" the other day, the exact emotion they might have experienced was exasperation, remorse or grief. Reading fiction books is a good way to increase our emotional vocabulary. Apart from that, we should pay close attention to how others behave and cautiously try to interpret the motivation behind their actions. Do not let fear prevent you from enjoying life but remember to remain ever vigilant for subtle signs of sociopathy in your closest surroundings, in order to prevent being caught off-guard and realizing once it's too late. Above all, take shelter in spiritual practice. If you manage to balance mindful contemplation and selfless action, you will achieve absolute control over the shape of your thoughts, words, and deeds. This is the most effective weapon against demoniac persons.

ON OFF-ROADING

Were we required to characterise this age of ours by any single epithet, we should be tempted to call it, not an Heroical, Devotional, Philosophical, or Moral Age, but, above all others, the Mechanical Age.
– Thomas Carlyle[26]

One beautiful autumn afternoon a man called Kevin went on a short hiking trip. The vivid colours of the foliage filled his heart with joy, as he was walking on a country lane that led through the woodlands. He found a secluded spot where he sat and attempted to meditate for a while. The growing serenity inside him was suddenly broken by a distant growl. Not even a minute had passed by when a group of men on quads and motorbikes appeared from around the corner. Kevin was not the only one that was disturbed by their unexpected intrusion. The infernal noise coming from their vehicles made the spirits of the forest cry in pain.

***

Over the last two decades or so, we have witnessed a growing interest in pursuing off-roading activities. Many men decide to buy vehicles such as jeeps, pickup trucks, quads or dirt bikes and drive on rural, unpaved roads, tracks, and paths. What is motivating them to take a drive off the beaten track? The hobby in question is without a doubt one of many modern substitutes for masculine heroism. It allows men to experience a feeling of thrill and a rush of adrenaline. Driving their vehicles gives them a sense of control and accomplishment when they get to where no one has ever been before. Others perceive off-roading as an opportunity to kill time or to prepare for survivalist situations. In my opinion, however, off-roading is one of the most environmentally damaging and pointless recreational activities. In this short essay, I am going to point out some of its darker sides and explain why I think that off-roading in the wilderness should not be allowed.

Mountains, forests, and other natural environments of (more or less) pristine beauty, are places where we rest and reconnect with our inner selves. The artificial rumble of the combustion engine is the last thing we want to hear there. There is enough unhealthy noise in the cities; why, then, would we want to pollute the countryside with it? The noise caused by off-road vehicles is not only unpleasant to our ears – it scares off wild animals and disrupts their diurnal cycles. Furthermore, the inevitable emission of

---

26   T. Carlyle, *Signs of the Times* (1829).

exhaust fumes drastically reduces air quality in formerly pristine habitats. Driving in the wilderness causes long-lasting damage to the landscape: soil displacement and compaction may leave hiking trails impassable. This is also linked to the sedimentation of streams. The excessive input of mud, sand, clay, and pebbles into water has a dramatic impact on aquatic ecosystems. The continuous deposition of sediment means that less space is available for animal and plant life. Light penetration is reduced, thus affecting the efficiency of the plants' ability to photosynthesise. Last but not least, off-road vehicles damage plants and spread noxious and non-native weeds into wild habitats.

Is it worth destroying our natural environment just to have some childish fun, then? A vast majority of adult men never grow up. They replace their toy cars with mechanical gadgets, but they never change on the inside. They become obsessed with cars, motorbikes or quads – often to the point where they prioritize them over relationships with other human beings. They may use elaborate excuses and justifications for behaving in such a way, but in the end these are just immature hobbies. Besides, owing to the cult of speed and convenience in our modern society, a lot of people are so used to comfort that the idea of walking instead of driving is inconceivable to their modern minds. Therefore, I am convinced that using off-road vehicles for recreational purposes should be completely banned in forests and mountains.

ON HIKING

The feats of audacity, risk, and conquest as well as the disciplines of the body, the senses, and the will are practiced in the immovable, great, and symbolic mountain peaks and lead men to the realisation that all in man is beyond himself.
– Julius Evola[27]

Far, far away, somewhere in the mysterious land of Svíþjóð[28], a man named Thorsten was ascending a mountain. His hair shone brightly in the afternoon sunlight. Thorsten, being a lion-hearted warrior of herculean frame but also a well-known researcher of ancient traditions, perceived the ascent as a terrific opportunity for strengthening his own body and spirit. The lonely, dome-shaped peak was illuminated by the warm glow of the westering sun. It loomed out of the wild and desolate moorlands, from which, suddenly and with a plaintive cry, a lone buzzard rose up high in the sky. Thorsten trod incessantly through the treeless, barren slope, strewn with erratic boulders. With every step he took, he grew stronger in his struggle against the mountain.

***

Going on a hike is the perfect alternative for mindless and environmentally destructive off-roading. Even a short excursion to the nearby hills will help you burn extra calories, improve your respiratory system and build strength in your muscles (especially of the lower body). Besides these (and many other) ways that hiking can improve your physical health, the activity in question has proven to be beneficial on a psychological and emotional level. Numerous studies confirm that trekking in nature has a positive impact on our attention span. The reasons for this are simple – we are forced to tread carefully and concentrate on our steps, otherwise we risk falling or even injuring ourselves. Furthermore, deep in the wilderness our senses are no longer bombarded with so many stimuli. Activities such as listening to enchanting birdsong, observing the fabulous shapes of the clouds moving across the blue sky, or admiring the beauty of pristine, wooded landscapes, effortlessly capture our attention. As long as we don't attempt to photograph everything around us (as explained in my essay on alienation), exposure to natural environments will tremendously

---

27   J. Evola, *Meditations on the Peaks* (Rochester, VT: Inner Traditions, 1998), p. 23.

28   The Old Norse name for Sweden.

increase our attention span, reducing mental fatigue and stress at the same time.

The key aspect of hiking is verticality. An ascent is a psycho-physiological form of purification, and its different stages resemble rising from the lower to the upper parts of the body. As we begin to climb the mountain, we gradually rise above the impure and hectic elements of day to day life. On the steep slopes, we push our muscular stamina to its ultimate limits. Finally, at the peak of the mountain, the crisp air of the heights cleanses our thoughts, sharpens our senses, and broadens our mental horizons. The absolute stillness that haunts the mountain heights is utterly terrifying to the spiritually impoverished athletes of our days, for it breaks the spell of their feverish mania for ceaseless activity and noise. Their approach to hiking is overwhelmingly quantitative – they conquer the silent mountain peaks just for the sake of setting new records. Completely oblivious to the goal of inner, spiritual realization, clad in expensive and fashionable sportswear, determined to prove their own athletic proficiency, they march toward the peaks like lifeless machines. The problem with the modern man is that he no longer pays any attention to what is invisible to the senses and to what does not produce immediate gratification or income. Thus, his interest in hiking is of a purely physicalistic nature.

As we can see, the impoverished forms of heroism, such as off-roading and competition-oriented trekking are devoid of any spiritual significance. The alternative is mindful hiking, which combines action and contemplation. How does it work? Before we set out from home, we define a clear goal of connecting with the more-than-human world on our trip. This includes contemplating the natural beauty of our surroundings, but also recognizing the metaphysical importance of the mountains.

Traditionally, many peaks were considered holy and regarded as the abodes of the gods. Their majesty, hermetic inaccessibility, and proximity to the heavens inspired feelings of awe and reverence. In ancient Greek religion and mythology, Mount Olympus was believed to be the legendary home of the principal deities of the Greek pantheon. Jupiter was worshipped in the Alps at the Great St. Bernard Pass, where a temple dedicated to him (he was known there as *Jupiter Poeninus*) was erected during the reign of the emperor Claudius. Vosegus, depicted in Celtic art as a huntsman, was a tutelary deity of the heavily forested Vosges mountains (*Vosego silva*) in eastern Gaul. Mountain peaks and prominent hills, symbolically associated with permanence and immovability (which are traditionally masculine, solar principles), were sometimes sites of royal and political power. Such was the case with Dunadd in Scotland, the coronation site of the early medieval kings of *Dal Riada*. The Hill of Uisneach was the mythical navel of Ireland (comparable with *Axis Mundi*), where according to *The Book of Invasions* the earliest partition of the island took place.

A mindful hiking trip resembles a pilgrimage in the sense that we set off with an intention of seeking inspiration, healing, and tranquillity in what lies beyond us. The calmness of the heights brings our inner selves closer to the primordial state of unity with the Earth. As we experience a fleeting glimpse of metaphysical reality there, we slowly realize that nature is full of living, sentient beings. The mountain peaks teach us humility and help us strengthen our connection with the divine. This is a powerful antidote for wistfulness and existential despair.

ON FORESTS

And into the forest I go, to lose my mind and find my soul.
– John Muir

An old Norwegian man called Theodor was picking mushrooms in the early hours of the morning. In his left hand, he carried a large wicker basket. A narrow path, cushioned by a patch of damp, spongy moss, led through a mist-covered woodland glade situated in the middle of a coniferous forest. The birds were chirping loudly and the woodpeckers were drumming on the trees continuously. Amidst the withered ferns, golden chanterelles and chestnut-brown boletes were fearfully hiding from human sight. Theodor, being a sensitive, deeply spiritual person, practised compassion toward all living beings, however; he avoided picking too many mushrooms, or mushrooms that were too young, because he wanted to give them a chance to replenish in time for next autumn's harvest.

***

Many people do not consciously think about the crucial importance of trees for our life on Earth. Our existence would not be possible without forests, for they produce most of the oxygen that humans and other living organisms breathe. They also regulate the way our natural environment functions. They have a tremendous impact on climatic factors such as temperature, wind, precipitation, soil, and noise, to name a few. Since the dawn of humanity, we have been venturing deep into forests in order to extract timber and firewood. Edible mushrooms, herbs, berries, and wild animals have nourished our bodies and kept us alive. However, the dwellers of concrete jungles are so detached from nature that they can think of forests only as a commodity. Once the modern man becomes ensnared in the illusory cult of civilizational progress, he begins drowning deeper and deeper in the cesspool of materialism, until all his noble qualities become atrophied. In his arrogance, he morally justifies deforestation as long as it generates income.

In every pre-Abrahamic, Indo-European culture from Ireland to India we can find a plethora of evidence of sacred reverence for trees. In the ancient times, forests and woodlands were perceived as enchanted places, alive with visible and invisible sentient beings such as elves, fairies, and dryads. Many religious rituals and ceremonies took place in secluded groves with old trees. The gods in the Sumerian *Epic of Gilgamesh* were supposed to dwell in the great cedar forest of the Zagros mountains of Iran. The

Avestan scriptures mention the major battle that occurred near the "White Forest" (*spaēitita razura*). It is suggested that the whiteness of the forest may represent either the pistachio groves of Iran[29] or the birch forests north of the river Jaxartes (Syr Darya). Interestingly, the ancient Iranians were probably among the first peoples to introduce codified laws related to forest management and tree protection. Herodotus reports that during his military expedition to Greece, Xerxes found a beautiful plane tree that he decided to decorate and put under the care of a guardian. Their sacred reverence for trees can be seen in some reliefs at Persepolis, which depict cedar and cypress trees. The cypress, being a strong and resilient evergreen, symbolizes vitality, immortality, and grandeur. It is the tree of life that bears a certain resemblance to the Norse *Yggdrasil*.

Many centuries ago, Europe was covered with endless forests. Unfortunately, the march of civilizational progress has led to trees being cut down in the hundreds of millions. In Ireland, deforestation has gone so far that the image of the Emerald Isle being covered with anything other than grasslands and bare hills has survived only in folklore from the distant Celtic past. The sense of sanctity of trees was central to the beliefs of the ancient Celts. Vast woodlands were frequently personified and protected by tutelary deities, such as Arduinna of the Ardennes Forest or Abnoba of the Black Forest. The Brehon Laws in early medieval Ireland classified trees and shrubs into groups of economic worth and protected them from being injured or cut down by imposing penalty fines on the culprits[30]. The seven noble trees (*airig fedo*) were: oak, hazel, holly, yew, ash, pine, and apple trees. The second category consisted of the so-called peasant trees (*aithig fedo*): alder, willow, hawthorn, mountain ash, birch, elm, and wild cherry trees. Lower yet in the classification were the scrub trees (*fodla fedo*): blackthorn, elder, spindle-tree, whitebeam, strawberry tree, aspen, juniper. Finally, to the least valuable class (*losa fedo*) belonged: bracken, bog-myrtle, furze, bramble, heather, broom, wild rose. Study of tribal names and place names throughout the Celtic world reveals an enormous richness of names etymologically derived from trees. One of the seven noble trees, yew (*eburos*), being an evergreen, was considered a symbol of longevity and immortality. On the other hand, its poisonous qualities are also well-attested in Celtic mythology and Roman sources. Julius Caesar wrote that king of the Eburones, Catuvolcus, committed suicide by poisoning himself with an

---

29   A. Hambartsumian, *The Sacred Aryan Forest in the Avestan and Pahlavi Texts*, Iran & the Caucasus, vol. 13, no. 1, 2009, pp. 125–130.

30   For more detailed information about this classification, please refer to the paper: F. Kelly, *Trees in Early Ireland*, Irish Forestry Journal, Nov. 1999.

extract from the yew tree[31]. Examples of names related to yew included: *Eburākon* (York), Eburones (a Gaulish tribe), *Eochaill* (Youghal in County Cork, Ireland), and *Eburobriga* (Avrolles, France).

Classical authors inform us that the esoteric doctrine of druidism was taught in secluded oak groves (*drunemeton*). Pliny the Elder describes a ritual, in which druids clad in white robes climbed a sacred oak, used a golden sickle to cut down the mistletoe growing on the tree, and sacrificed two white bulls[32]. Sacred reverence for oaks, intricately linked with the cult of the thunder god, was also common to other European cultures. The ancient Greeks worshipped Zeus in the sanctuary at Dodona, where a holy oak tree grew, until it was cut down when Emperor Theodosius declared Christianity the official religion of the Roman Empire. Oaks were also consecrated to Jupiter, the chief deity of ancient Romans. *Corona civica*, a military decoration given to a soldier who had saved the life of a fellow citizen, was a wreath made of oak leaves or acorns. Aulus Gelius explains the choice of this tree in his *Attic Nights*[33], by stressing the life-supporting role of oak trees. Indeed, acorns were not only used to feed pigs, but they were also roasted and ground into flour. The oak wood was famed for its strength and durability. From a more metaphysical point of view, however, those adorned with oak crowns were protected by the divine Jupiter. The poet Ovid mentions that an oak wreath was set above the emperor Augustus' door[34]. Thor, the thunder god, appears as the central figure in Germanic religious beliefs. There is a strong association between the worship of Thor and sacred groves. According to the 8th century *Life of Saint Boniface*, a sacred oak consecrated to Thor was located in a grove somewhere in the land of the Hessians. Another forest dedicated to Thor was known as *Caill Tomair* ('Thor's Wood'), located near Norse Dublin. More traces are found in several place names in Anglo-Saxon England. Examples include: *Thunres leah* in Hampshire, *Thunreslea* in Essex, and *Thursley* in Surrey. The place-name element *leah* means 'grove' or 'woodland glade'.

The purpose of the above historical review was to demonstrate the extent to which ancient Indo-Europeans venerated trees and woodlands. Their highly respectful attitude to nature directly disagreed with the

---

31   Caesar, *Bellum Gallicum*, 6.31.

32   Pliny the Elder, *Naturalis Historia*, 16.95.

33   Aulus Gelius, *Noctes Atticae*, 5.6.12.

34   Ovid, *Fasti*, 1.608.

Abrahamic worldview, and Abrahamic missionaries committed heinous acts of vandalism at sacred groves in an attempt to eradicate heathen religions. The sanctity of forests has been forgotten in the modern world. It is high time to change the way we see and interact with them. First and foremost, modern ecology has to be grounded in a higher, metaphysical tradition. Had we perceived woodlands as sacred spaces alive with personality, rather than just mere clumps of green matter, we would have never allowed the massive deforestation of entire countries to take place. For this reason, the felling of oaks, yews, ashes, and other culturally important tree species has to be reduced to a minimum. Off-roading in the wilderness should be banned. Furthermore, we have to start thinking of littering in forests as equal to leaving rubbish in churches and temples.

Indo-European pagans of the present times should be encouraged to visit forests frequently, not just for the sake of seeking mere relaxation or pursuing physical activities such as cross-country running (although both are productive ways of spending one's time), but also to reconnect with the divinity present in nature. This can be achieved through solitary meditative practice or group rituals and offerings. In contemporary Baltic paganism, worshipping deities in old, sacred groves is not a re-enactment of the past, but a living tradition. Heathens from other parts of Europe should follow the example of their Baltic counterparts and *make forests great again*, to paraphrase a popular slogan.

ON UNIQUENESS

Every one loves his country, his manners, his language, his wife, his children; not because they are the best in the World, but because they are absolutely his own, and he loves himself and his own labours in them.
– Johann Gottfried Herder[35]

One December night, a man called Arminius was travelling through Austria by train. Hallstatt, an ancient archaeological site, was his final destination. He had chosen an almost empty compartment, where his only companion was a young lady sleeping by the window. The train was rushing through a howling blizzard as she breathed softly in her undisturbed sleep. The alabaster paleness of her slender fingers bore a close resemblance to the snowy peaks that loomed in the distance. The girl's intricately braided blonde hair had a unique, platinum shade. Arminius glimpsed at her face two or three times, although he could not see it clearly enough in the darkness. As they were approaching a small train station somewhere in Upper Austria, the train slowed down and the light of street lamps started peering into the carriage through the window, illuminating her countenance with ephemeral light and shadow play. The train stopped and a complete silence fell over the compartment. She woke up suddenly and opened her azure blue eyes. The girl fixed her gaze on Arminius and smiled charmingly. The man was flooded with a sudden wave of genuine warmth which beamed from her radiant countenance. In that very moment, he was ready to protect her from anything that could have blemished her angelic uniqueness.

***

Today, it is often said that all human beings are equal. The media constantly remind us about the policy of equal opportunity in employment and education. Some people, driven by an excess of wishful thinking, go as far as to reject any qualitative and differentiative judgments. According to them, there is no such thing as *good* or *bad* art. They also claim that men and women are basically the same, and that their gender roles are a social construct, which should ideally be abolished in favour of total freedom in this area of life.

In our modern society, underdogs are encouraged to take pride in their mediocrity, ugliness or minority status, whereas strong, beautiful, and

---

35   J. G. Herder, *Outlines of a Philosophy of the History of Man* (London: Hansard, 1803), p. 18.

healthy individuals are never allowed to say that some people are better than others, or that some moral stances are objectively superior to others. They are not allowed to celebrate and preserve their identity and heritage, their most cherished traditions and customs. Today, displaying a protective and knightly attitude towards women is frequently perceived as something highly inappropriate, sometimes even oppressive. In this way, modern men are literally prohibited from proving their worth and honour. How can they fulfil their innate, biological roles if their natural instincts are nipped in the bud? The same applies to modern women: a young girl who expresses her willingness to have many children and to become a housewife is often met with mockery, laughter, and a lack of understanding.

In general, human life is a constant tension between *losing* your extraordinariness and *preserving* it. An individual is exposed to a multitude of different personalities during their lifetime. This causes an internal conflict: *should I conform and be like them or should I maintain my uniqueness?* The more conformist and agreeable behaviours you exhibit, the more successful you are in the eyes of modern society. Naturally, a certain dose of individualism is allowed and even tolerated. You can wear different brands of clothing, you can have your favourite musical bands, you can be an animal rights activist, you can even vote for different political parties. You can do whatever you want and be whoever you want, as long as you pay taxes and keep your mind busy by agreeing upon solutions that *they* offer you. But real individualists, i.e. those who attempt to undermine the foundations upon which modern society is built, are subjected to persecution (or in the best case – they are ignored). They do this because they realize that the decline of traditional life philosophy, which is deeply rooted in transcendence, is the main source of all problems – and that we need to look for more radical solutions which would allow us to live more authentic lives.

Contrary to some optimistic prognoses, the society of tomorrow will not be a harmonious and peaceful amalgamate, in which the diversity of particular groups or individuals would be respected and honoured. A grey mass of mindless robots in human skin is what probably awaits us.

A traditionalist notion of uniqueness has nothing to do with conceited bragging or hatred of other groups. Rather, it's a gesture of respect for yourself and for your ancestors who struggled and fought to maintain their true identity and distinctiveness from others. Only a traditionalist society based upon the hierarchical system of *varnas* creates conditions in which all individuals can thrive without having to sacrifice their own personality for the sake of social conformity. For example, in the bygone world of

Tradition, gifted introverts performed important functions of bards, priests, seers, and healers. Today, in an overly-extroverted, materialistic civilization which values only incessant external activity, such people are treated as social outcasts. Their extraordinary skills are tamed by the public education system which aims to bring everyone down to one low level. Homeschooling your children is the only sensible way to preserve their creativity and nurture their unique hobbies and talents.

From the windy Aran Islands of Ireland, to the mighty Ural Mountains in Russia; from the majestic fjords of Norway to the sunny islands of Greece – you shall find beauty and uniqueness therein. Every European country has its own traditions, customs, and beliefs. In every European region, you shall find distinctive human phenotypes and languages. When I look at the tall, blue-eyed, blonde Swedes (although one valiant, Anglo-Saxon gentleman has also infiltrated their ranks...) who gather around the ancient burial mounds in Gamla Uppsala, in order to celebrate Winter Solstice, I have nothing but admiration and respect for the richness of their culture. When I watch how a stocky Bavarian shepherd, dressed in a traditional garment inherited from his grandfather, follows the doleful cries of lost sheep, I have nothing but admiration and respect for his traditional way of living. When I stand on the white cliffs of Dover, looking wistfully at the stormy sea, I am reminded of the legendary sunken land of *Ys*. I wonder, what will happen to us? Will we throw ourselves into the sea, to drown in dull greyness? Or will we stand tall on the top of the white cliffs?

As long as I live, I will not allow the former to happen. Neither should you.

ON BREVITY

True brevity of expression consists in a man only saying what is worth saying, while avoiding all diffuse explanations of things which every one can think out for himself.
– Arthur Schopenhauer

Have you noticed that those who have nothing important to say are the ones speaking the most? They escape from their own emptiness by drowning it in a constant babble. You can see such talking heads rambling on television or on the Internet. They are often journalists or politicians, who cover up their lack of intellectual depth and substance with the lengthiness of their speech. A man of few words is a noble soul and he speaks only when has something important and wise to communicate. For what is the point of chattering about trivial and meaningless matters?

As you may have noticed, my book is written concisely. I try to articulate my thoughts clearly and in a way that would not bore my readers. The sole function of the poetic threads, sporadically woven into the narrative, is to convey a specific atmosphere and message. My essays are not supposed to provide you with entertainment or a mere opportunity to pass the time. I respect your precious time, therefore I do not want to waste it on meaningless, inconclusive speculations. Instead, I offer you sensible solutions, tips and practical advice.

There are several other reasons why I advocate for brevity in writing and speech. In our turbulent times, in which we are bombarded with an overload of information, in which *everyone is afraid to be forgotten,* true wisdom is buried beneath heaps of trash. Thus, the only way to break through information pollution is to communicate your ideas in a brief yet informative manner. However, I need to stress that conciseness of expression should be combined with a profound insight into subjects or ideas. Otherwise, we run the risk of falling into the trap of mediocrity and triviality.

ON ALIENATION

There are reasons to believe that the identification with frenzied and elementary rhythms produces forms of 'downward self-transcendence', forms of sub-personal regression to what is merely vital and primitive, partial possessions that, following moments of violent intensity and quasi-ecstatic outbursts, leave one feeling even more empty and estranged from reality than before.
– Julius Evola[36]

One March evening I went on a lone walk to the nearby woods. The full moon hung high in the cloudless night sky, illuminating the Earth with her silvery presence. I sat on a mossy rock and meditated in silence for a while. The stillness of my surroundings was broken by an owl's call. Later on, I noticed that the moonlight created a peculiar path of pale lightness amidst the birch trees. It was a very primeval experience. It made me wonder: how many people are still capable of noticing such small details?

***

We are so detached from our natural environment that we cannot feel any spiritual connection to the trees, stars, quiet rivulets and misty clouds. Our eyes can see them, but our soul is blind to their beauty. Everything is becoming more and more horizontal, and less vertical. People no longer look at the sky; everybody's gaze is fixed on their own electronic device. It is important to remember that what we describe is not just a disconnection from nature, but also from transcendence, from anything that is imperceptible to the senses. In the beginning of the Silver Age, the prehistoric man had been thrown into the world of becoming and experienced a progressive alteration of his own consciousness. No longer in a direct communion with the divine, as he gazed at the starry night sky, he was struck by a feeling of his total insignificance and loneliness in relation to the vastness of the universe. Death, illness, toil, and despair began to torment him. The connection with transcendence was temporarily restored thanks to the wisdom of the venerable sages, who taught mankind powerful techniques of spiritual practice. Already back then the connection was loose, however, as the spiritual practice required much concentrated effort to silence the constant restlessness of one's mind. As time went by, man has only fallen lower and lower from his pure and undifferentiated primordial state of being.

---

36   J. Evola, *The Youth, the Beats, and Right-Wing Anarchists* (1968).

Since then, instead of finding refuge in spiritual practice, we have designed sophisticated ways to distance ourselves from the world around us. A typical citizen of our *brave new world* no longer perceives reality directly through his eyes and ears. He lives in a cyberspace of indirect experience. To explain what I mean, I would like to briefly elaborate upon my perception of live performances. One who attends rock or metal concerts can see a crowd of detached individuals, who intoxicate themselves with alcohol in order not to feel lonely, and to be able to digest the art presented onstage. The Dionysian-like experience of rock music differs enormously from people's mundane, daily existence, as its ecstatic rhythm and loudness shatter the boundaries of rational individuality. In black metal, the most extreme form of rock music, we find a powerful fusion of atavistic screams and chaotic noises that threaten to swallow the Apollonian sun of rational order. In other words, black metal (oftentimes regarded as a form of *anti-art*) opens the portal to the naked truth about our inner despair that we try so hard to conceal with comforting images of entertainment. Most people who go to such concerts prefer *not* to think too much, therefore they numb their senses with alcohol, drugs and... photography!

Yes, photography. Instead of experiencing music directly (all they need is a pair of ears and eyes...), they take photos of the band or film the entire performance with their phones or digital cameras. They do not concentrate on the present, real and tangible moment, but create an artificial, indirect memory of it.

The same can be said about tourists who admire the beauty of cultural or natural heritage not with their own eyes, but through the veils of digital cameras. Furthermore, a lot of people take photos with the primary intention of posting them on social media, in order to receive instant gratification. The direct experience of the present is lost in the intemporal sea of lenses and screens. Can we really blame others for taking a keen interest in photography? Photography as a derivative form of painting shields us from previously described feelings of metaphysical nausea, which can surface when we perceive reality directly. However, I believe that a tactic of constant avoidance is counter-productive in the long run. We may feel safer under the shelter of mechanical images, but we never confront the problem head-on. Waking up from this peaceful slumber and recognizing our part in nature through conscious spiritual practice is an absolute necessity for personal development, lest we turn into mindless, robot-like creatures. Moreover, those who rule the world would love us to go with the flow of such technological pipe-dreams, so that we stop questioning anything.

As we see, our disconnection from nature is rapidly accelerated by progress. The boundaries between relatively unspoiled countryside and crowded cities are becoming increasingly blurred owing to the process of urbanization. New technological advancements and facilities are indiscriminately accepted by the masses, which only care about immediate convenience, regardless of the long-term consequences. Our children are no longer taught how to identify plant and animal species. Instead, since their early years they are encouraged to watch cartoons and to play games on different electronic devices.

It's high time for us to find the optimal balance between us and nature. The first step towards this goal is to limit our excessive attachment to modern technology. Introducing a few Internet-free days into your monthly schedule will help you realize that you won't miss out on anything while you are away. On the contrary, you will most likely notice that going offline is the key to enhancing your productivity and improving your concentration. The next vitally important step is to change the way you use modern technology in relation to your surroundings. In order to get closer to a direct perception of reality, you can leave your digital camera at home when you go on a trip. We put ourselves under strong, psychological pressure to take photos. Many people are under the spell of a common misconception that a holiday excursion not documented through the lens of a camera is a holiday without memories. This is a myth, and according to scientific studies, taking photos may even impede our memory[37]. Despite not having cameras, people of the past had far better memory than we do. Why do we still feel overly anxious and guilty when we leave the camera at home? Why are we still tempted to live our entire lives through a plastic screen? Cast away the shackles of technology, cut off your dependence on artificial stimulation.

We may recognize the enormous significance of choosing to live closer to nature, but we must also keep in mind that unless this essential step is taken simultaneously with a genuine desire to tighten our bond with the divine, our efforts will yield unsatisfactory results. Through conscious and systematic involvement in spiritual practice, as well as by the attentive study of the ancient scriptures, we gradually lift the veils of illusion and suffering. Ultimately, we find ourselves sheltered from the chaotic, unpredictable world of becoming. Those who master the art of being present in the material world, whilst having their mind fixed in transcendence at the same

---

37   Henkel, L. A., (2014). *Point-and-shoot memories: The influence of taking photos on memory for a museum tour.* Psychological Science, 25(2), 396-402.

time, acquire great inner tranquillity and stabilization.

ON SECRECY

Telling someone something he does not understand is pointless, even if you add that he will not be able to understand it. If you have a room which you do not want certain people to get into, put a lock on it for which they do not have the key. But there is no point in talking to them about it, unless of course you want them to admire the room from outside! The honourable thing to do is to put a lock on the door which will be noticed only by those who can open it, not by the rest.
– Ludwig Wittgenstein[38]

A warm June day was coming to an end. A young lady called Freya was slowly riding on a white horse, admiring the beauty of her sylvan surroundings. The forest was gradually darkening in the waning light. Only a few sun-flecks caressed the path with their golden fingers. The primeval stillness whispered to Freya's imagination, reminding her of ancient druidic groves that once dotted the Welsh landscape. Unbeknownst to her, she was being observed by a giant stag who stood, motionless, on a nearby hillock. The animal's broad antlers looked majestic in the crimson glow that peered through the foliage. There was an inexplicable air of mystery in Freya's deep blue eyes – perhaps she was daydreaming about meeting her noble knight next week? Her meditative mood was abruptly interrupted by noisy movement in the foliage. Freya halted the horse and made her stand completely still. She looked around. Out of the corner of her eye, she espied the stag languidly returning to a thicket. Freya instinctively wanted to take a photo of the animal, but on second thought she decided to look at it with her own eyes instead. The softly diffused light flickered faintly on the reddish-brown fur as it faded away into the distance. Freya thought that such a rare encounter with the stag was too magical to be shared with a wide circle of friends. She decided that it would be more appropriate to keep it a secret, not to be revealed to anyone except her beloved one, the noble knight Urien.

***

We are living in very strange times. A photograph or a video recording of burial mounds at Gamla Uppsala in Sweden can be shared with someone living on the opposite side of the globe in the blink of an eye. It is estimated that approximately one million digital self-portraits are being taken every day to be posted on social media. Our modern times are characterized by an ever-growing obsession with sharing tiny and usually

---

38   L. Wittgenstein, *Culture and Value*, 7-8.

insignificant details from our daily lives. The advent of social media has caused a completely normal part of social interaction to get out of control. The Internet has given us a golden opportunity to express ourselves without any limitations, but we have wasted this chance on reinforcing our narcissistic, self-aggrandizing tendencies.

A lot of people complain about the lack of privacy in our modern times and blame politicians for this state of affairs, yet, at the same time, they voluntarily expose themselves on social media. I deeply believe that we should consider changing our attitude towards sharing. There is a time and a place for participating in gregarious interaction and exchange, but it should be counterbalanced with time spent alone. The latter does not imply the absence of other people in one's physical proximity, either. It simply means that we should celebrate the present moment without having any digital witnesses. We should refrain from taking photos and filming, especially when we are confronted with something radically unusual and different from our daily experience. We should aim for secrecy of special moments. For example, taking a hike deep into nature and observing wildlife is a great occasion for learning how to keep such precious moments private. This makes us more likely to appreciate the present moment, as it's experienced only by us (unless we make an exception for a few beloved ones, which is totally understandable) and no one else. Such intimate experiences cause gratitude for the blessings that fate has bestowed upon us. Moreover, it is a well-known fact that confidentiality within a small group strengthens bonds between its individual members. The same is true for couples, marriages, and siblings.

In today's globalized world, it is becoming increasingly difficult to find quiet and serene places where few people have been before. I strongly encourage you all to step off the beaten track every once in a while and explore areas beyond your immediate surroundings. An old hornbeam forest, a tranquil birch grove on a gentle hillock, a ramshackle barn in an overgrown field – let us remember and frequently visit such secluded spots. I believe that every person should have their own favourite, secret place and only show it to their beloved one or a close friend. I think it's an excellent way to forge meaningful bonds with persons dear to your heart. My secret place is located on a hiking trail, high in the mountains. At first glance, there is nothing exceptional here, but in the late afternoon, especially in the autumn, the undergrowth changes its colours and you can see a beautiful play of light and shadow on the forest path.

Another specific trait of the modern world is that everything is becoming increasingly open and accessible to the masses. Even though instant access to knowledge on the Internet makes learning easier and more convenient, the democratization of every possible piece of information through technology stands in radical opposition to the traditional world, which clearly distinguished between exoteric and esoteric knowledge. The exoteric surface of philosophical or religious doctrines was available to all, whereas the esoteric depth was transmitted orally by a spiritual teacher to an exclusive group of initiates. For instance, classical writers report that the Celtic doctrine of druidism was secret, taught in secluded places such as woodland glades and caves, and the novices had to memorize a great number of verses before they could be initiated. The modern policy of equal opportunity does not take into consideration that individual persons differ considerably in their comprehension of higher, sacred knowledge. It is important to understand that the two paths were not contradictory, they were just two possible perspectives of looking at this particular spiritual tradition. Exotericism was chiefly concerned with an outward action and ritual, while on the esoteric path the emphasis was placed on knowledge itself.

It is indeed unfortunate that we have to navigate a world that has forgotten such simple truths. Modern people living under the reign of mediocrity continually babble about equality, tolerance, and open-mindedness, not realizing that these are just empty, meaningless slogans. Such slogans could only be promoted in a degenerated form of civilization, in which clueless, hollow zombies live a life devoid of any profound, metaphysical significance. Let us not despair, however, for there is still hope. Even the tiniest acts of revolt against the modern world matter. As we disassociate ourselves from modern trends (such as the above-mentioned mania for over-sharing on social media), we begin to understand that a different, more meaningful life is possible. Let us cultivate close and healthy relationships with a few trusted friends, instead of seeking the attention and acceptance of people who don't even bother to get to know us well.

ON DARKNESS

It cannot be seen, cannot be felt,
Cannot be heard, cannot be smelt.
It lies behind stars and under hills,
And empty holes it fills.
It comes first and follows after
Ends life, kills laughter.
– J.R.R. Tolkien[39]

A starless November night. An old wooden cabin, somewhere in the middle of a deep and dark forest. Cold rain is beating upon the roof. Inside, a hooded figure sits at the oaken table. Only the dim glow of a candle illuminates his mysterious, sullen countenance, partially hidden in the gloom. The candle is placed in a wooden, drakkar-shaped vessel which is hanging from the ceiling. An icy wind whistles through the knotholes in the planks, creating a draught that makes the candle flame flicker slightly. There is a furnace in the corner of the room, but it seems that the man has decided not to build a fire. Sudden pops and cracks in the wood create an illusion of some ghostly presence. Everything in this forlorn place is cloaked in the veils of strange murkiness.

***

We have banished darkness from our modern world. What have we gotten in return? Millions of brightly flashing screens, light bulbs, and street lights. Everything is predictable, mechanical, and dull. Perhaps such conditions make us feel safer and more comfortable, but nothing truly magnificent has ever been born inside one's comfort zone. Darkness sparks your imagination and brings some uneasiness and discomfort into your life. The fear of the unknown plays a major role in our perception of the night. When it's dark, a mere bush or gnarled root can look like a terrible troll. A walk in the forest at midnight is an unforgettable experience. In the history of armed conflict, many battles and sieges were won precisely because of surprise attacks conducted under the cloak of night. In the Iliad, Odysseus and Diomedes carry out a night raid on the Thracian camp. They manage to slay king Rhesus and steal his horses[40]. In the Old English poem *Beowulf*, it is under nightfall that Grendel – a monstrous creature from the swamps – attacks the men sleeping in a great mead-hall called Heorot. He is

---

39   J.R.R. Tolkien, *The Hobbit*, chapter 5.

40   Homer, *The Iliad*, X, v. 465-514.

described as *sceadugenga*, literally: shadow-walker[41].

In the past, human activity was mostly confined within the hours of daylight. Even in today's electrified world, people tend to become more emotional, reflective, and prone to intrusive and anxious thoughts once darkness falls. One of the most evocative images of eventide grief can be found in an early Welsh poem called *Canu Heledd*. Cynddylan was a prince from the Romano-British kingdom of Powys. He and his brothers were slain in battle against the Angles from Northumbria. The poem is a lament of Cynddylan's sister, Heledd, who mourns the death of her kinsmen and the dilapidation of her home:

Cynddylan's hall is dark tonight

without a fire, without a bed.

I will weep for a while, afterwards I will fall silent.

Cynddylan's hall is dark tonight

without a fire, without a candle.

Except for God, who will give me sanity?

Cynddylan's hall is dark tonight

without a fire, without a light.

Grief comes to me because of you.[42]

On the other hand, the absence of daylight can shelter you from danger – being less visible, you may hide much more easily. This was especially true for women in the past. One of the Old English words for darkness – *heolstor* – literally means "hiding-place". Night is also the time when humans sleep, allowing their bodies to regenerate, but many animals lead either crepuscular or nocturnal lives. Although the perception of darkness in our culture is predominantly negative, in reality night-time is neither

---

41   *Beowulf*, v. 702.

42   J. Rowland, *Early Welsh Saga Poetry: A Study and Edition of the Englynion* (Cambridge: D.S. Brewer, 1990).

good nor bad, like all natural phenomena.

When I was a child, power outages happened more frequently than they do today. I always rejoiced at moments when suddenly everything turned black. Unless I had been reading or writing prior to the blackout, I didn't even feel the need to illuminate the darkness with candlelight. I would sit by the windowsill and stare at the pitch-blackness outside. Such disruptions of routine are feared by ordinary people, who are so used to modern technology that they don't even bother to think what would happen if these facilities ceased functioning properly. Moreover, they seem to have no problem with constantly increasing light pollution, to which I would now like to draw your attention.

The sight of the night sky dotted with myriads of stars was taken for granted by our ancestors. In his famous work *Patterns in Comparative Religion*, Mircea Eliade argues that the sole act of contemplating the *heavenly abode* evokes a religious experience. The observer is confronted with something infinite, transcendent and substantially different from his earthly existence[43]. However nowadays, especially to those who live in cities, looking at the Milky Way is more like a myth or an anecdote told by grandparents or great-grandparents. Not only does too much artificial light obscure the night sky's numerous celestial bodies, but it also negatively impacts ecosystems by confusing light-dependent patterns of animal activity. Our streets and motorways are cluttered with glowing neon lighting, billboards, and many other illuminated signs which demand our constant attention. To make things worse, the light of street lamps often literally trespasses on people's properties, shining on their walls and in through their windows.

How can we fight light pollution? I think that people should generally go to bed earlier (whenever possible) and accomplish most of their tasks during daylight hours. As soon as it gets completely dark, let us light candles (instead of using electricity) and pull the curtains together so that no light escapes outwards through the windows. Those who own a car should avoid driving after dusk. Last but not least, motion-sensor lights should be installed on porches to avoid leaving glaring outdoor lights switched on all night long. In today's digital world, over-illumination caused by blue light from electronic screens has a detrimental effect on one's sight and general health. One reason why people suffer from insomnia and other sleep disorders is because they use electronic devices shortly before going to bed.

---

43   M. Eliade, *Patterns in Comparative Religion* (London and New York, 1958).

One possible solution is downloading applications that adjust the colour temperature of electronic screens according to the time of the day, as well as installing proper ambient lighting. However, I suggest a more radical, yet highly effective alternative. As I said before, in traditional societies, eventide has always been the time for rest, relaxation, and reflection on the day that has passed. What is stopping you from lighting up a candle and meditating for a while in semi-darkness, at least for a few moments before you sink into sleep? You no longer have to be socially active. Conversations and messages can wait until tomorrow. If you try this simple evening ritual, you will quickly notice how it helps to aid restful and undisturbed sleep.

It is beyond any question that we should establish a sensible balance between darkness and light. In order to succeed in doing so, we need to significantly reduce light pollution and practice a number of nightly rituals, such as stargazing, quiet meditation, and adopting healthy sleep patterns. However, we must take into consideration several obstacles that might hinder us from fully implementing the aforementioned attitudes. These can include ruminations, anxious thoughts, and a general inability to concentrate properly on the here and now. I explain how to solve these issues in the subsequent essays.

ON SOLITUDE

The mind is sharper and keener in seclusion and uninterrupted solitude. No big laboratory is needed in which to think. Originality thrives in seclusion free of outside influences beating upon us to cripple the creative mind. Be alone, that is the secret of invention; be alone, that is when ideas are born.
– Nikola Tesla

A young Swiss girl named Claire is sitting at the kitchen table drinking coffee. It is late afternoon and the sun is shining through the floral pattern, Sezession-style silk curtains. Claire has been home alone today and exceptionally productive since the early morning. She has finished her new landscape painting, written her school assignments and carried out various household chores. Still, she has managed to make time for a longer break during which she went for a pleasant walk in the woods. Now, as the day is coming to an end, Claire is observing the gentle light and shadow play in the kitchen. She does not mind being alone; in fact, she loves solitude and always yearns for it. Sometimes, Claire sits for hours at her windowsill and meditates upon the clouds passing by. Then, inspired and rejuvenated by the beauty and serenity of nature, she proceeds to create highly imaginative art.

However, the very same girl struggles to develop and maintain close friendships with her peers at school. Claire's unwillingness to participate in group work is perceived by her teachers as deliberate selfishness. The truth is different, though. Claire, as an introvert and a highly sensitive person, dislikes superficial socialization. Noisy chatter and small-talk completely drain her of energy, forcing her to take a nap after school. She does not like group work because she is more intelligent and has more brilliant ideas than her peers. As long as the public education system will continue to be based on intellectual and social conformity, individuals like Claire will not get the opportunity to develop their extraordinary talents to their full potential.

***

Our modern society is obsessed with extraversion and gregariousness, which are said to be prerequisites for socio-economic success. We are told at school and through the media that an individual who is inclined to associate with or be in the company of others is also more likely to become successful in life. Our children are intentionally discouraged from pursuing solitary hobbies or even just doing things on their own. Moreover, there is a popular trend among "busy" parents to schedule a lot of extracurricular activities for their children. Although such a policy certainly gives the latter plenty of opportunities for socialization and self-realization, it completely neglects the child's need for solitude and parental closeness. In the end, this counter-productive trend leads to serious developmental problems amongst children, such as low self-esteem or anxiety.

Like I said in my essay about uniqueness, homeschooling your children is the only sensible way to preserve their creativity and nurture their specific hobbies and talents. Home is like a sanctuary for homeschooled children, a safe place where they can learn at their own pace, with their uniqueness respected – especially if they are gifted individualists like the Swiss girl mentioned in the first paragraph. A lot of people criticize home education, arguing that sending your offspring to a public school is the *only* way they can learn social skills. In reality, socialization at school (by which I mean spending most of your childhood and adolescence in same-aged classrooms), does not emulate social interactions in the real world. Children need to interact with people of various ages and backgrounds and they also need to learn how to deal with different, complex social situations. Contrary to popular belief, when homeschooling is done properly it cannot be equated with sheltering a child and forcing it to live in a bubble. Thoughtful parents provide their children with an abundance of extra activities like meet-ups with other homeschooling families, field trips, visits to museums, ballet classes, music lessons, group sports and so forth.

Solitude is a blessing that gives us tranquillity and solace. It enables self-examination, an insight into our thoughts and motives – a prerequisite for the development of self and spiritual growth. Since most people are afraid of contemplation these days, they avoid being alone. In their desperate efforts not to feel lonely, people develop a tendency to seek various distractions to occupy their attention. They may throw themselves into a social whirl: getting intoxicated with alcohol or drugs every weekend at parties, or extensive oversharing on social media (for the sake of instant gratification), are two of the most popular ways to *forget* about oneself. Others, in an attempt to escape from their own internal despair, may turn all important metaphysical questions into one big, sarcastic joke. In any case, there is a high price to pay for such choices. Without introspection, people wander aimlessly through their meaningless lives, pursuing shallow goals like a career, money and material possessions, bodily pleasures and so on. In the end, they die without ever *living* first.

There is a widespread belief that seeking restorative solitude means abandoning worldly concerns and goals in favour of an anchorite lifestyle. Nothing could be further from the truth. A healthy balance between time spent alone and time spent with others can be attained through very simple means. Even if you live in the middle of a big city, you only have to close the door of your room and sit in silence for a while. You may then listen to some quiet music, read a book, or meditate upon the subject of your choice. One such brief moment is far more fruitful than hours spent scrolling purposelessly through social media. One reason why a lot of people today experience terrible loneliness, is, paradoxically, because during waking hours they are *never* alone with their own thoughts, and at the same time they lack close relationships in real life. They are connected and interact with each other *all day long* through social media. The Internet gives them the dangerous illusion of experiencing meaningful socialization, while in reality they are just interacting with their electronic devices. No matter how real online conversations may feel, they are entirely confined within the digital world. Thus, they can never replace face-to-face meetings.

In our modern world, we are told that interacting with hundreds of individuals from different backgrounds and ethnicities is something perfectly normal. However, we have lived in small tribal communities for thousands of years, and our nature is still tribal: we are not supposed to maintain daily contact with such a vast number of people, many of whom are complete strangers to us. This is the root cause of social anxiety. I would therefore advise you to re-evaluate your friendships and ask yourself a few simple questions: which people that I interact with make me miserable? Are there any relationships in my life that are not worth continuing? Do both of us benefit spiritually and morally from talking to each other? Do I really need so many "friends", who don't even know my real *self*? Do not be afraid to break all those superficial bonds – it's for your own good. Learn how to love solitude and from then on only seek meaning and authenticity in your relationships.

ON SILENCE

Men talk to escape from themselves, from sheer dread of silence. Reflection makes them uncomfortable, and they find distraction in a noise of words. They seek not the company of those who might enlighten and improve them, but that of whoever can divert and amuse them. Thus the intercourse which ought to be a chief means of education, is for the most part, the occasion of mental and moral enfeeblement.
– John Lancaster Spalding[44]

Somewhere in the ancient kingdom of Rheged[45], crepuscular shadows slowly enshrouded a peaceful meadow where delicate gossamers floated in their celestial drowsiness. A fair poetess sat on a large moss-grown boulder in a birch copse. Following the footsteps of her mythical predecessor Taliesin[46], she sought inspiration among the soothing serenity of trees. She gazed heavenwards, at the setting sun, hidden behind mackerel clouds which were ablaze with a crimson glow. No sound could be heard, except for the rustling of foliage in the copse caused by a gentle breeze. Even the birds had ceased singing, as if enchanted by the very last rays of the setting sun. At the edge of the meadow ran a small rivulet. As the fleecy clouds above flushed delicately, the clean, silver flow was painted with an amalgamate of ochre and woad. The lustrous whiteness of her cheeks soon assumed the roseate hue of hearty joy. The Earth was quiet again, sunken into her twilit dreams.

***

We are living in the age of loudness. Never before have we lived in a world so polluted with noise. This is mainly due to rapid technological progress and the process of urbanization. Even the countryside is no longer as peaceful and quiet as it used to be one hundred years ago. The encroachment of machines not only spoils formerly pristine natural habitats, but also deprives us of a chance to enjoy the reinvigorating qualities of silence. Cars, motorbikes, quads, tractors, chainsaws, and many other modern machines promise us a paradise of speed and efficiency, but

---

44   J. L. Spalding, *Aphorisms and Reflections* (1901), p. 155.

45   Rheged was a post-Roman Brythonic kingdom located in what is now Galloway and North Cumbria. It existed from the late 5th century to the early-mid 7th century.

46   Taliesin was a semi-legendary Cumbric bard living in the 6th century.

at the same time throw us into the hellish pits of an unbearable cacophony of noise. Is our health and sanity really worth sacrificing for the sake of accomplishing our daily tasks faster?

The omnipresent intrusion of noise has not omitted our households, either. Even though the modern man locks himself in soundproof fortresses to protect himself against the noise outdoors, he still seems to enjoy living in a cesspool of loudness. Listening to music through headphones or earphones has become an inseparable part of many young people's lives. Although it is convenient and pleasurable, constant exposure to deafening sounds blasting directly into our ears damages our hearing and concentration. In the age of endless chatter, people are terribly afraid of outer and inner silence. As an illustration of this point, we need not look further than at those who fall asleep with their television set or radio turned on. Others cannot imagine their morning routine without these devices humming in the background. Many parents let their infants and toddlers watch television, but according to scientific studies such early exposure to media and background noise may negatively impact the child's language development, attention span and short-term memory[47]. Moreover, the unhealthy spirit of extreme gregariousness in many of our contemporaries (and their preference for being in the very centre of noisy crowds rather than seeking solitude) is a telling sign that the modern man deliberately avoids the supposed discomfort of silence. Ignorant to the restorative nature of stillness, fully immersed in the ocean of clamorous gibberish, he seems to be a hopeless case.

Silence, this time understood figuratively, is uncommon in our digital age on the Internet. The immense popularity of self-expressive media such as blogs or video blogs proves that everyone is talking and writing, but few are willing to take a step aside, read a book, or listen to someone wiser than themselves. In the dense jungle of the Internet, only those who shout the loudest, with their dishonest click-bait headlines and dramatic, attention-seeking behaviours, seem to thrive. The cult of hollow celebrities and fake, conceited, unqualified "lifestyle gurus" swallows the last bits of authenticity and truthfulness. According to the post-Vedic scripture of Bhagavata Purana, in our dark age of Kali Yuga, *one who is very clever at juggling words will be considered a learned scholar*[48].

---

47   Madigan S, Browne D, Racine N, Mori C, Tough S. *Association Between Screen Time and Children's Performance on a Developmental Screening Test.* JAMA Pediatr. 2019;173(3):244–250.

48   *Bhagavata Purana*, 12.2.4.

To paraphrase Julius Evola's famous saying[49]: let us leave modern men to their *bread and circuses*, and let us only be concerned about one thing: to live in montane strongholds of tranquillity and mindfulness, rising high above the incessant racket of the crowds. The preliminary stage of the journey toward those metaphorical abodes of serenity is to reduce our exposure to external noise. Do we really need to wear earphones for the greater part of our day? I can partially understand people who listen to music in this way while commuting, or while performing tasks that require total concentration (studying, reading, etc.) in noisy environments. Likewise, those who are involved in sport activities may increase the effectiveness of their training by listening to their favourite tracks through earphones. These are understandable, though not ideal cases. My main point, however, is that the modern man deliberately bombards his own ears with high-volume sounds in situations and circumstances that do not justify it. For instance, there is absolutely no need to impede our concentration and general health while reading or studying in quiet environments, strolling in nature, or falling asleep. The same can be said about frequently attending loud rock or metal concerts – intemperance in this area of life may negatively affect our well-being in the long run.

Shouting, making loud exclamations, and speaking in a raised voice have their time and place in the realm of human communication. How often do we raise our voices unnecessarily, though? This is especially the case with many parents, who yell at their children with the intention of enforcing discipline. This creates a vicious cycle of completely ineffective verbal abuse – the child misbehaves, the parent reprimands it with harsh, loud words, the child's reaction is usually the opposite of what the parent was hoping for, so the latter becomes even more aggressive (which often escalates into physical abuse). Living in such a toxic, stressful environment can lead to severe emotional trauma and negative changes in brain structure. The ancient Stoics recommended cultivating the virtue of firmness, which in this context is understood as the quality of not being soft, but not completely impenetrable, either. There is absolutely no need to resort to hysterical, ear-piercing screams in order to appear convincing. Let us introduce placidness into our households and workspaces. Another good custom to adopt is eating communal meals in silence. There is no doubt that dining together creates and strengthens bonds between individuals who gather at the table and share their thoughts and daily experiences with each other. Communal meals are crucial for healthy family relationships. In Zen

---

49   From *Revolt Against the Modern World*: "let us leave modern people to their truths, and let us only be concerned about one thing: to keep standing amid a world of ruins."

Buddhism, however, monks and nuns practise mindful eating in silence:

While eating perfect quietude prevails; the dishes are handled noiselessly, no word is uttered, no conversation goes on, and all their desires are indicated by folding and rubbing their hands. Eating is a serious affair with them[50].

If we master the art of doing only one thing at a time, we will quickly notice how focusing entirely on the task or action at hand considerably enhances the quality of our lives. Exclusive concentration on what we eat and how we eat it makes the process of dining more enjoyable and gives our bodies proper nourishment. Let us put aside conversations and distracting text messages – they do not require our immediate attention. Those who are struggling with dispelling the mist of a wandering mind may try mantra meditation[51] shortly before dining. Our bodies also yearn for a moment of sweet silence.

Those who live in cities should consider moving to the countryside at some point in future. As has been said previously, it is indeed unfortunate that even rural areas can no longer be considered safe havens for individuals who seek sweet repose of the mind. No matter how severe the modern man's detachment from nature will ever become, our innate need for halcyon woodlands and meadows will never leave us. As explained in my essays on hiking and forests, the sanative power of mindful strolls in nature fills our hearts with a sense of joyful balance. Exposure to stillness puts a stop to the constant chatter that pollutes our minds.

An excess of silence is not ideal either, unless one is well-trained to cope with it. In Alexandra David-Néel's famous book *Magic and Mystery in Tibet*[52] we learn about recluse Buddhist monks (*gomchen*) who voluntarily spend entire months and years either in specific abodes of meditation (*tsams khang*) located in the vicinity of a monastery or in remote cave dwellings high in the Himalayas. On could wonder how these anchorites do not become insane owing to the unbroken silence which surrounds them on all sides for miles. However, these men are thoroughly trained and prepared for seclusion. Advanced yoga techniques (such as *tummo* – inner

---

50   D. T. Suzuki, *An Introduction to Zen Buddhism* (New York: Grove Press, 1964), p. 122.

51   More on this in my essay on concentration.

52   A. David-Néel, *Magic and Mystery in Tibet* (New York: Dover Publications, 1971).

fire meditation[53]) and various other spiritual exercises make their solitary retreat evoke feelings of "voluptuous sweetness", as David-Néel puts it in her book. With this exception in mind, an excess of silence is still generally harmful to our well-being. People cannot live in a psychological vacuum. If we don't stimulate the formation of new synaptic connections in our brain, we begin slowly drifting backwards to earlier stages of development. Therefore, we can't just avoid the world and shut ourselves in echo chambers, no matter how much corruption and degeneracy we witness around us. On a positive note, there is still beauty and hope to be found even in the darkest moments of Kali Yuga, provided one can open their mind and see beyond superficial forms. Last but not least, too much silence in human relationships is probably just as bad as loud arguments happening every day, if not worse – indifference can sometimes hurt more than a violent confrontation.

---

53   One can read more about this technique in the aforementioned book *Magic and Mystery in Tibet*. *Naljorpas* (dwellers of remote caves) use this method, in order to raise their body temperature significantly. This allows them to endure severe, freezing winters on the snow-covered slopes of the Himalayas. I may add that a Dutch extreme athlete Wim Hof has invented a set of breathing exercises inspired by *tummo* meditation. Those who are interested in taking cold showers should definitely look it up.

ON DAYDREAMING

[In the Modern West] it is taken for granted that anyone who is not in a state of agitation and who does not produce much in a material way must be an "idler".
– René Guénon[54]

A young Danish lady called Luna was rhythmically rocking back and forth on a swing that hung from an old oak tree. A single strand of her silver-blonde hair glimmered evanescently in the aureate sunlight. Every time the swing reached its highest point, Luna's closed eyelids were gently touched by the warm, autumnal breeze which peered through the branches. A hint of a faint, charming smile flickered across her luscious, cherry-coloured lips. She was clearly experiencing a moment of pure bliss. There were earphones in her ears, so she was probably listening to one of those ethereal, dreamy bands like Cocteau Twins. The ground was strewn with fallen leaves that rustled softly in a zephyrean dance. Luna was slowly waking up from her meditative state. Her deep blue eyes resembled the sunless waters of the sea at dusk.

***

Why is daydreaming frowned upon in our modern society? As the French philosopher René Guénon would have said, the modern man is living under the tyrannical reign of Quantity[55]. To the vast majority of our contemporaries, any activity that does not produce immediate quantitative, measurable results is perceived as a waste of time. This is the reason why dreamlike fantasies during waking hours are widely regarded as unproductive. If only the modern man shifted his attention from what is immediate to his senses, he could open the gateway to the realm of creativity, problem-solving, and endless possibilities. A healthy dose of daily daydreaming is essential to the mental well-being of intellectual and artistic types. For the former, a short-term detachment can be a perfect opportunity to conjure up brilliant ideas and effective solutions to problems. As regards the latter, I think it is obvious that daydreaming is highly beneficial to the process of creating art. In Virginia Woolf's novel *To*

---

54   R. Guénon, *The Crisis of the Modern World* (Varanasi: Indica Books, 2007), p. 114.

55   Guénon perceived history as a downward devolution from Quality toward Quantity. His *magnum opus The Reign of Quantity and the Signs of the Times* is a criticism of modernity from such perspective.

the Lighthouse, we can find an accurate depiction of introspective musings: "losing consciousness of outer things…her mind kept throwing up from its depths scenes, and names, and sayings, and memories and ideas, like a fountain spurting"[56].

For those whose daily tasks do not revolve around the direct application of intellectual and creative aptitudes, the practice of daydreaming can also prove to be advantageous. It is especially effective when the labour being done is mind-numbing and tedious, as is often the case in the psychologically-estranging capitalist mode of production. Sometimes one's mind stays on a manual task better when it is partially distracted, either externally (e.g. music playing in the background) or internally (daydreaming). That being said, it is important to stress that an excess of daydreaming has a detrimental effect on our productivity and concentration. Therefore, when indulging in such activities, we need to tightly hold the reins of self-control and moderation, lest we lose touch with reality. In the next essay, I am going to elaborate on why I think that every major undertaking requires deep concentration.

---

56   V. Woolf, *The Selected Works of Virginia Woolf* (Hertfordshire, England: Wordsworth Editions, 2007), p. 359-360.

ON CONCENTRATION

Do the things external that fall upon you distract you? Give yourself time to learn something new and good, and cease to be whirled around. But then you must also avoid being carried about the other way. For those too are triflers, who have wearied themselves in life by their activity, and yet they have no object to which to direct every movement, and, in a word, all of their thoughts.
– Marcus Aurelius[57]

Somewhere amidst the green hills of County Mayo in Western Ireland stood a partially dilapidated round tower. The building had been hastily abandoned a few months prior during a Viking raid. The first floor had been plundered and left in a state of disarray. The raiders had either neglected or had not been able to reach (perhaps because the ladders had been taken away by the defenders) the upper part of the tower, for it remained intact. On the uppermost storey, a renowned musician called Conchobar played the harp whilst the birds were sweetly singing in the warm, eventide air. A light breeze blew through the narrow window, quietly ruffling Conchobar's golden hair. Not even the arrival of a small swallow on the windowsill could break the musician's absolute concentration.

***

In the digital age, staying focused on our goals requires much effort and perseverance. Distractions assail us from every direction. Every single day we are continually bombarded with intrusive news, phone calls, notifications, and advertisements. Our minds are cluttered with completely inessential bits and pieces of information that steal our precious time and attention. Studies show that our attention spans are getting shorter and shorter due to the omnipresence of digital distractions[58]. The modern man's preference for ever-accessible instant gratification has markedly affected his cognitive abilities, turning him into a lazy, unfocused, child-like creature, struggling to delay an immediate convenience for the sake of a greater reward in future. Being a chronic procrastinator, he rarely reaches his maximum potential.

Considering these unfavourable conditions, drawing up an effective plan

---

57   Marcus Aurelius, *Meditations*, II, 7.

58   A. Gazzaley, L.D. Rosen, *The Distracted Mind: Ancient Brains in a High-tech World* (Cambridge, MA: MIT Press, 2016).

for combating these obstacles is not an easy task. Although modern interconnectivity breeds distraction, it is still possible to retake control over our focus without quitting social media and the Internet altogether. In the following paragraphs, we are going to discuss several practical and reliable methods that facilitate the process of attention restoration.

First and foremost, it is always a good idea to get busy every once in a while. This doesn't mean frenetically occupying yourself with incessant activity, something characteristic of the vast majority of our contemporaries. We should define explicit and attainable goals to work towards on a daily basis. They don't have to be overly ambitious (at least in the beginning), but it would be beneficial if they were serious enough to become our greatest and most urgent priorities. The next step is to devote a considerable amount of time to them, so that we have a regular schedule to keep. Whenever our mind wanders to something more pleasant and rewarding (such as taking a quick glance at notifications on social media), we must react immediately and get our thoughts back on track. Let us think of our daily challenges as soldierly duties that must be executed, regardless of external circumstances or our current mood. The ancient Stoic philosophers, inspired by the rigid resolve of Roman legionaries, rightly emphasized the accuracy of this analogy. What the modern man clearly lacks is strict discipline that is maintained without regard for pain or pleasure. As Lord Krishna says in the *Bhagavad Gita*: *for him who has conquered the mind, the mind is the best of friends; but for one who has failed to do so, his very mind will be the greatest enemy*[59]. The mind is like a precious treasure that requires constant vigilance against undesirable forces that can potentially compromise our sense of duty.

One reason why so many individuals fail to set realistic priorities and carry out duties is because they pay too much attention to what others think or say. In the age of mindless conformity, the shape of our dreams and goals is strongly influenced by peer pressure and dominant trends and fashions. People are afraid to think outside the box. Their desires and aspirations fluctuate with each passing season. Grounding our lives in an authentic spiritual tradition is the best remedy against the chaos within us.

In order to improve our concentration and achieve a sense of inner peace, we should get into a habit of daily meditation. There are many benefits of this ancient practice. From a biological point of view, the sympathetic nervous system, which is responsible for the body's reactions to stress, shuts down during meditation. In our current high-stress civilization, many people live in a state of chronic anxiety that eventually

---

59   *Bhagavad Gita*, 6.6.

leads to serious problems such as physical and mental exhaustion, lowered immunity, and insomnia. Meditation pacifies the sympathetic nervous system, aiding rest, relaxation, and digestion, which are in turn responsibilities of the parasympathetic nervous system. Scientific studies also indicate that meditative practices lead to a reduction in the activity of the default mode network, a large-scale brain network associated with daydreaming and ruminations (which are not good in excess). Finally, empirical research proves that meditation can increase one's attention span and other cognitive abilities[60].

From a secular point of view, meditation consists of breathing exercises and, in some cases, repetitive affirmations. As was proven above, these activities are beneficial to our physical and mental well-being. However, the benefits can be maximized if our practice is taken to a higher, religious level by repeating mantras. Mantras are sacred words, discovered by the ancient seers who experienced the divine directly, that produce vibrations at certain frequencies and ranges. They are not just mere mental focus points, but reflections of universal energies. Chanting a mantra strengthens the union with our eternal self (*atman*) and liberates us from the hypnotic glamour (*maya*) of the material world. The sound vibrations are transmitted throughout the body, bestowing their healing properties upon us. At the end of the book I explain how to practice meditation properly.

Although meditation techniques and mantras are now almost exclusively preserved in the scriptures of Sanatana Dharma (Hinduism) and Buddhism, there is nothing to suggest that similar methods didn't exist in other pre-Abrahamic, Indo-European cultures. Many ancient Greek philosophers stressed the importance of self-examination. Some of them were taught and initiated by Egyptian sages and Persian *magi* who might have been familiar with these techniques. In his work *On Nature*, the pre-Socratic philosopher Parmenides described a mystical inner vision that he had experienced himself[61]. The report of his vision is not very dissimilar from what *yogis* of India experience in their meditative states. Plotinus, a 3rd-century Neoplatonic mystic, argued that *henosis* (a state of oneness with the divine) can be achieved by turning wholly within, purifying one's consciousness from external sensations and dualistic patterns of thinking. The Celtic deity Cernunnos, depicted on the Gundestrup Cauldron (comparable to the representation of the Vedic god Shiva on the Pashupati

---

60   R. Sheldrake, *Science and Spiritual Practices* (London: Coronet Books, 2017), pp. 23-49.

61   L. Johnsen, *Lost Masters: Sages of Ancient Greece* (Honesdale, PA: Himalayan Institute Press, 2006).

Seal) and on the Reims Altar, is seated in the lotus position (*padmasana*), possibly indicating a meditative state. Since the late eighteenth century, scholars have highlighted the close similarities between the Celtic druids and the Vedic *brahmanas*. This view was supported by the Hellenistic writers of the Alexandrian School, who considered druids to be sages parallel to those known to us from Greek, Egyptian, Persian, and Vedic traditions. It is also possible that various meditative techniques could have developed in ancient Europe independently from Oriental influence. After all, the yearning for self-analysis and inner stillness is something universal, not exclusive to the peoples of India or Tibet.

Meditation is not the only way to effectively improve our concentration. The effects of regular exercise on emotional and mental well-being have been studied scientifically. Participation in sport stimulates the production of serotonin and endorphins in brain, which enhance mood, alleviate symptoms of anxiety and depression, and boost our attention span. Indeed, exercise forces us to be present in the moment and focus fully on the movement of our body. Athletes and sport coaches often stress the importance of proper focus during sport competition. Just like in every other area of life, being distracted undermines our chances of achieving success.

According to the attention restoration theory (formulated by Rachel and Stephen Kaplan in the 1980s[62]), the ability to concentrate is improved after spending time in natural environments. Thus, we should consider working out in nature (at least two or three times a month). For example, we can combine hiking with calisthenics or forest walking with cross country running. Logs, tree branches or rocks can serve as natural training equipment, while obstacles like gnarled roots, slippery stones, and treacherous ditches require our constant attention. After completing the workout, it is essential to slow down and just admire the beauty of our surroundings. Examples of passive activities that can potentially boost our attention span include meditating by the riverside, admiring the majestic beauty of distant mountain peaks or listening to enchanting birdsong. The rejuvenative power of nature cannot be underestimated.

---

62   R. Kaplan and S. Kaplan, *The Experience of Nature: A Psychological Perspective* (Cambridge: Cambridge University Press, 1989).

ON PATIENCE

Beware the fury of a patient man.
– John Dryden[63]

A young artist called Vicky was slowly walking among the ruins of an old church, situated on a windswept clifftop. The sea-dampened walls of the medieval building provided no shelter from the trickling rain. Vicky was a renowned painter, known for her magical depictions of northern landscapes. Since the early afternoon, she had been waiting for the Sun to be roused from the arms of Morpheus. Although no signs of life could be seen anywhere in this tenebrific, godforsaken realm of perpetual fog and everlasting rain, something was beginning to clear up in the sky. As time went by, low clouds gradually began to dissolve. Here and there, clearances appeared, revealing the pale azure tint of the sky. Vicky's patience had finally been rewarded, and she could joyously begin her *plein air* session.

***

The German philosopher Arthur Schopenhauer once expressed his annoyance at impatient individuals who drum their fingers on the table when they are waiting for someone. If Schopenhauer were alive today, what would he say about the technology addicts of our times? What would he say about the millions of people desperately yearning for bits and pieces of instant gratification? Those who have carefully read all the previous essays presented in this book know that the world has embarked on a downward spiral in many different ways. The last negative trait of the modern world that needs to be addressed is the growing culture of impatience. Most of us probably fail to realize how the desire to seek short-term pleasure and to avoid pain (associated here with delay and anticipation) has become the basis of consumerism in the digital age.

Let us take the popularity of pre-orders as an illustration of my point. The idea behind this marketing strategy is that due to technological progress, people are becoming more and more accustomed to convenience and the immediate gratification of their needs. Video game, music, and movie producers cleverly exploit such psychological tendencies and dupe customers into ordering a product that has not yet been released. A few months before the release date, an atmosphere of keen anticipation is established by the means of promotional trailers and teasers. Some producers include additional physical items in the pre-order deliveries. This

---

63   J. Dryden, *Absalom and Achitophel*, I, v. 1005.

makes fans ready and willing to pay more for faster access to the product. From an ethical point of view, pre-orders are fundamentally dishonest, and I would encourage my readers to become vigilant of the temptation to purchase something earlier for the sake of instant gratification.

Nowadays, we are constantly told that patience and slowness need to be avoided at all costs, for – according to modern standards – they get in the way of earning money. A fast-paced lifestyle, money-making *ad infinitum*, career advancement, the acquirement of latest gadgets – these are the loftiest ideals of our current age. Multitasking, meeting deadlines, and producing immediate, quantitative results are preferred over slow and diligent work focused on long-term goals. Laziness and lack of drive are spreading like a plague, petrifying our minds. The aforementioned attitude is incompatible with the traditional world, however. How can the inorganic men of modern cities fully appreciate the hard work of a farmer, when all they have ever seen is the finished product, a loaf of bread ready to be purchased in a giant supermarket? When you are disconnected from traditional life, you are oblivious to the fact that every important task requires patience, diligence, and concentration. A highly specialized medieval artisan such as a goldsmith could have never been successful without them. Modern technology creates the illusion that spectacular results can be achieved with very little effort in a short time. Nothing could be further from the truth.

In my opinion, waiting for someone to arrive is a golden opportunity to exercise the virtue of patience and to reflect upon the complexity of life. Sit on a bench or a stone and just let your thoughts roam free. Your innermost universe is rich enough to provide you with numerous issues to ponder on. If anticipation often makes you feel anxious, you must realize that the amount of time you will have to wait is usually beyond your control. What is beyond our control should not disturb us at all. Do we get upset when apple trees do not bear fruit in winter? Of course not, since Mature Nature, a force beyond our power and control, decided otherwise. Why are you nervous about protracted waiting for a latecomer or a train, then? Have you considered the possible influence of external factors, such as illness, an accident or bad weather? When you realize that what is on the outside should not concern you at all, you will finally find peace of mind.

ON ANGER

Mankind is born for mutual assistance, anger for mutual ruin: the former loves society, the latter estrangement. The one loves to do good, the other to do harm; the one to help even strangers, the other to attack even its dearest friends. The one is ready even to sacrifice itself for the good of others, the other to plunge into peril provided it drags others with it. Who, then, can be more ignorant of nature than he who classes this cruel and hurtful vice as belonging to her best and most polished work?
– Seneca[64]

As the light darkened at dusk one November day, a wayfarer called Feardorcha was standing among the majestic ruins of Dún Aonghasa. The harsh wind was driving the rain horizontally, straight into the strider's face. He stood there motionless, gazing silently at the vast abode of Manannán mac Lir. It seemed as if the ocean's roars were being caused by a mirage of the wave-sweeping chariot drawn by Manannán's magical horse. The seething rage in the water and in the air had no effect on Feardorcha's calm countenance, however. His unwavering stature resembled the slabs of jagged limestone which stood upright outside the middle wall guarding the fortress against the unknown terrors coming from the ocean[65].

***

Whenever someone criticizes you, you should nip your initial, impulsive angry reaction in the bud and consider the nature of the one judging you. Find out whether they are a person of virtue and honour. Many people are

---

64   Seneca, *On Anger*, 1.5.2.

65   This introductory paragraph refers to Dún Aonghasa – a prehistoric promontory fort located on the Aran Islands off the west coast of Ireland. The fortress consists of four concentric walls made of dry stone. It is built on the top of a rocky cliff towering above the sea. Manannán mac Lir was the sea god in Irish mythology. His attributes include a magical boat or chariot known as Scuabtuinne ("wave sweeper") and a sea-borne horse named Énbarr ("froth"). The limestone slabs in question are a network of defensive stones (*chevaux de frise*) located outside of the middle wall of Dún Aonghasa. The fort had been inhabited since at least 1100 BCE. Those interested in learning more about the site and its curious history can read *A Study of the Fort of Dun Aengusa* written by the famous Irish antiquarian T. J. Westropp.

constantly deceived by their own false reasoning, for they are driven by strong emotions and wishes; whereas calm, well-balanced individuals are perfectly capable of judging matters from a neutral point of view. The former often live as if the world revolves around them, blaming everybody else for their own suffering. It should come to you as no surprise that people whose lives lack spiritual depth cannot handle any form of criticism. These types of people will attack you viciously, even if you begin talking about moral attitudes and virtues in general, without targeting them or being accusative. They cannot stand their own mediocrity; therefore, they hide their guilt behind a wall of wrath and hatred towards those who are above them, both morally and intellectually.

Contrarily, a man of wisdom is always open to justifiable criticism, for he sees it as the key to the gate of self-improvement. His feelings of guilt are immediately nipped in the bud, as he decides to change his ways and moral attitudes for the better. The suppression of unnecessary anger is one of the many virtues we should learn on our journey to perfection. Nature can or even should be our inspiration in this task. Sit by a quiet rivulet and look at the current. The water flows peacefully, undisturbed by stones and pieces of wood that may block its way. We should always strive for such calmness. From classical sources, we know that Celtic warriors would taunt and provoke their enemies before engaging in combat. Moreover, there were special units of Celtic mercenaries called *gaesatae*, which were comprised of berserkers who went into battle naked. Their nudity was supposed to intimidate and unnerve enemies. However, you should rather be like an exemplary Roman legionary who dispassionately enters the fight and only takes orders from reason. Do not let anything external break through the mighty walls of your tranquil and equanimous mind. For anger, even during war, opens the path to weakness, just like every notion caused by strong emotions. Disdain for mindless, petty persecutors and resolving to enact revenge upon them, is a sign of a great soul and noble spirit.

The sage is never angry at those who have gone astray. If possible, he shows them their errors and points out that they have strayed from the virtuous path. However, when he sees a solid wall of ignorance and battlements swarming with hosts of false notions, he turns back and leaves. Similarly, every sensible army commander would resign from besieging a heavily defended stronghold, if the assault would only cause the slaughter of his own troops. People are often mistaken in their opinions and actions, for they live contrary to nature and reason. Your impact on others' lives is not unlimited. However, it is perfectly possible for you to become an example to follow, by leading a virtuous life that is devoid of unnecessary anger and unreasonable notions.

Finally, I would like to clarify by adding that in some situations and circumstances, anger can, in fact, lead to positive outcomes. Rage can drive people who have been (often dangerously) inactive to action. They seek revenge or bare their teeth as a display of fierce and threatening aggression. Anger, just like fear, can manifest itself as a primitive mechanism for physical survival. Moreover, the prolonged suppression of emotions, including wrath, has a detrimental effect on one's mental health. Considering the evidence, it is unreasonable to completely ignore the emotion in question and perceive it as black or white. However, just because angry behaviour may occasionally produce a good outcome, it does not mean that we should deliberately evoke such emotions. Only a man of Stoic self-mastery is able to combine rage and calmness, and still emerge victorious over himself.

Julius Caesar, in his *Gallic War*, wrote the following about the chariots of the ancient Britons:

> In chariot fighting the Britons begin by driving all over the field hurling javelins, and generally the terror inspired by the horses and the noise of the wheels are sufficient to throw their opponents' ranks into disorder. Then, after making their way between the squadrons of their own cavalry, they jump down from the chariot and engage on foot. In the meantime their charioteers retire a short distance from the battle and place the chariots in such a position that their masters, if hard pressed by numbers, have an easy means of retreat to their own lines. They combine the mobility of cavalry with the staying power of infantry; and by daily training and practice they attain such proficiency that even on a steep incline they are able to control the horses at full gallop, and to check and turn them in a moment. They can run along the chariot pole, stand on the yoke, and get back into the chariot as quick as lightning.[66]

Isn't this a powerful image of self-control? In a figurative sense, the horses are our emotions, and the chariot is our reason. Without moderation and control, emotions are like restless horses running free. A skilful charioteer holds the reins of reason and is able to forge his wrath into a mighty weapon. Even on a steep slope where the danger of crashing into self-destruction looms, he remains remarkably calm in his anger. Enemy armies tremble and flee in terror when the thundering sound of his chariot

---

66   Caesar, *The Gallic War*, translated by Carolyn Hammond (Oxford: Oxford University Press, 2008), p. 86.

fills the air. The real battle is fought within the mind, and the inner victory manifests itself externally through the divine-like manner of heroic deeds.

ON INDIFFERENCE

It is not our part to master all the tides of the world, but to do what is in us for the succour of those years wherein we are set, uprooting the evil in the fields that we know, so that those who live after may have clean earth to till.
– J.R.R. Tolkien[67]

The average citizens of the Western world are taught to have compassion for animals, for starving children in economically underdeveloped countries, and for victims of wars in remote places all over the world. Yet, at the same time, they adopt an attitude of uttermost indifference to many problems that occur in their own countries. Such persons, despite outwardly projecting an image of themselves as an empathetic activist, are often very selfish in their daily conduct. Nowadays, it's simply fashionable and politically correct to be an advocate for global peace and prosperity. Those who do not hold such views, and instead prefer to focus on protecting and improving the well-being of their closest kinsmen and compatriots, are labelled as insensitive, selfish or even hateful persons. Although many naïve people who are manipulated by politicians and the mainstream media may think otherwise, it is not possible to care about the entire world. Likewise, it is impossible to love everyone. A friend to all is a friend to none. If we want to make a positive change, we need to start by changing ourselves and helping our close friends realize their full potential. Moreover, there is nothing wrong with choosing to care about those who look like us and think like us. We should never feel guilty for prioritizing local issues. Aiming for the self-preservation of the group we belong to is the opposite of selfishness. Any argument to the contrary is totally invalid.

The modern world is full of terribly selfish people. The spirit of global togetherness (extensively promoted in the name of eliminating prejudices and boundaries) cannot conceal this fact. In the prosperous countries of the West, where easily obtainable individual comfort facilitates selfish and decadent lifestyles, it has become the norm not to care about anything past the end of one's nose. The favourite watchwords of the modern man are: *après nous, le déluge* ("after us, the flood") and *Man lebt nur einmal* ("you only live once"). As long as he has his artificial paradises (gadgets and an Internet connection are now the preferred ways of escaping reality), they are content. They are deeply concerned about the survival of orangutan populations in rainforests (because it's fashionable to care about animal

---

67   J.R.R. Tolkien, *The Lord of the Rings: The Return of the King* (London: HarperCollinsPublishers, 1991), p. 185.

rights), but at the same they rarely think about their next-door neighbour. Enamoured with personal freedom and fighting for social justice, they remain indifferent to the idea of having children and protecting their own cultural heritage.

Let us break this spell of indifference. Instead of dedicating our time and energy to remote causes, we should rather take a closer look at our immediate surroundings. There is always something to be done and improved in our local community. Although the news are usually full of depressing headlines, we should not ignore them altogether. Millions of people live in a parochial bubble of seemingly blissful ignorance. An attitude of deliberate ignorance can prove dangerous in the long run. On the other hand, those who read the news every day are more likely to be affected by the negativity (primarily the undesirable quality of *tamas*) that causes depressive and anxious thoughts. Therefore, one should balance pursuing information with periods of abstinence from it. On another note, it is a good idea to catch up with our friends and family members every once in a while, in order to see whether they need our help and guidance. A relationship built on mutual trust and respect makes it easier for either party to open up and speak without the fear of being judged or blamed. When it comes to online interactions, it is important to support like-minded content creators, especially those who vigorously swim against the current of modernity. They need our words of encouragement and praise for their tireless efforts to change the *status quo* way of thinking. Instead of idly wasting our time on watching entertaining videos of cats and dogs (it is no exaggeration to say that this is what many people do on a daily basis, the same can be said about the obsessive interest in memes), let us actively seek valuable, intellectually stimulating articles, posts, and videos.

SUMMARY

The current age of dissolution does not provide much hope for a radical change in the socio-political structure of modern civilization. We must accept our limitations in this particular matter. Despite these adverse circumstances, attitudes of deep pessimism and quiet resignation have to be avoided, for they lead to even greater mental and spiritual atrophy within us. There is no other sensible choice but to actively resist the ongoing crisis. We have to ground our daily existence in the stability of spiritual tradition, so that our inner constitution remains unchanged even amidst the greatest upheavals. The purpose of my book is to show meaningful ways in which individuals who are inwardly detached from the insanity of modernity can still lead spiritually-saturated lives in radical opposition to the predominant trends and fashions. These practical solutions can be summarized as follows:

- Reduce your exposure to the unnecessary and unwholesome comforts of modern life. Beat addictions. Eat healthy, organic food. Consider taking cold showers.
- Introduce some form of physical exercise into your weekly routine.
- If you are a man, focus on developing a chivalric mindset that combines strength and courage with self-control and calmness.
- If you are a woman, strengthen your feminine attributes. Exhibit softness in your speech. Avoid foul language. Provide care and nurture to your closest ones. Grow long, beautiful hair. Avoid vain exhibitionism.
- Determine your *varna* using the descriptions provided in the book. Find a vocation compatible with your inner constitution.
- If you are a family-oriented person, prioritize having children and homeschooling them.
- If you are not a family-oriented person, prioritize finding a practical way in which you can contribute to the overall betterment of your folk. Master a traditional craft. Popularize and preserve old traditions. Become a counsellor or a teacher.
- Get rid of material possessions that do not uplift you spiritually or do not serve any practical function in your life.
- Avoid actions that place you in the undesirable modes of *rajas* and *tamas*.
- Increase your emotional awareness. Control the way you handle negative emotions.
- Take pride in your ancestral traditions and cultural heritage.
- Practice stargazing.
- Connect with nature through the meaningful activities of hiking and

forest walking.

- Balance socializing with like-minded people with invigorating days of solitude and silence.

- Learn the art of deep concentration. Practice daily meditation.

- Exercise the virtue of patience. Control your anger.

- Care about your local community, environment and like-minded friends.

APPENDIX A – HOW TO MEDITATE

The simplest ritual of secular meditation can be summarized as follows:

1. Sit in a quiet spot, devoid of sounds and sights that might unnecessarily agitate your mind. It can be either somewhere in your living space or in a serene, natural environment.
2. Close your eyes and make yourself comfortable.
3. Slowly put aside all negative thoughts, ruminations and anxieties. Do not be discouraged if you fail, but gather up enough determination to continue trying nonetheless.
4. Focus on your breath and on how the body moves with each inhalation and exhalation.
5. Continue for about 10 minutes or longer.
6. After you are finished, don't immediately open your eyes and rise. Sit still for a moment.

However, in order to fully experience the tremendous benefits of meditation, one has to repeatedly and quietly utter a chosen mantra. Mantras are sacred words (discovered by the ancient seers) which produce vibrations at certain frequencies and ranges. They are not just mere mental focus points, but reflections of the universal energies. The sound vibrations are transmitted throughout the body, bestowing upon us their healing properties. This practice has to be preceded by the above-mentioned breathing and concentration exercise.

For more information about mantras, please refer to the following works by Sri Dharma Pravartaka Acharya and David Frawley (Pandit Vamadeva Shastri), two knowledgeable Vedic gurus:

D. P. Acharya – *Sanatana Dharma: The Eternal Natural Way*
D. Frawley – *The Art and Science of Vedic Counseling*
D. Frawley – *Vedantic Meditation*

APPENDIX B – ESTABLISHING SACRED SPACE

It is important to arrange a small space somewhere in your house, purposely designed for spiritual practice.

1. Find a quiet spot in your home. It doesn't have to be an entire room. A small corner of the room is a good idea.

2. Clean and declutter this space.

3. Put a small wooden table or a shelf there.

4. Make the sacred space pleasant to your senses. Put some flowers in a vase. Bring some pine cones from the forest. Light up a candle. Put a rug on the floor.

5. Depending on your personal religious beliefs, try to get some images or figurines of the deities or holy symbols. You could also place some photos of your ancestors there.

6. Regularly purify the air in the sacred space with lavender or cedar smoke. When burned, these herbs can significantly improve your mood and alleviate some discomfort.

7. No arguments, noise or loud music are allowed in the sacred space. Try to avoid negative feelings and resolutions (e.g. anger or thoughts of revenge) while being there.

8. Use the sacred space for meditation, prayer, making offerings to the deities, or any other form of contemplative spiritual practice.

APPENDIX C – RECOMMENDED CULTURAL WORKS

BOOK RECOMMENDATIONS

The following is a list of books I wish to recommend to my readers Please note that the choice is quite personal, and I don't completely agree with the theories presented in *some* of these books, but they are all thought-provoking and worth reading.

The Celts

L. Alcock – *Arthur's Britain*
M. Aldhouse-Green – *Dictionary of Celtic Myth and Legend*
J. Caesar – *The Gallic War*
N. Chadwick – *The Celtic Realms*
B. Cunliffe – *The Ancient Celts*
B. Cunliffe – *Iron Age Communities in Britain*
P. Ellis – *The Druids*
M. Green – *Animals in Celtic Life and Myth*
I. A. Gregory – *Gods and Fighting Men*
I. A. Gregory – *Visions and Beliefs in the West of Ireland*
P. W. Joyce – *A Social History of Ancient Ireland*
C. Lowe – *Angels, Fools and Tyrants*
Mabinogion
A. MacBain – *Celtic Mythology and Religion*
A. Moffat – *Arthur and the Lost Kingdoms*
D. O hOgáin – *The Celts: A History*
T. F. O'Rahilly – *Early Irish History and Mythology*
S. Piggott – *The Druids*
C. Tacitus – *Agricola*
Táin Bó Cúailnge

The Germanic Peoples

M. Aldhouse-Green – *Bog Bodies Uncovered*
B. Bates – *The Real Middle-Earth: Magic and Mystery in the Dark Ages*
Beowulf
H. R. Ellis Davidson – *Gods and Myths of Northern Europe*
H. R. Ellis Davidson – *The Lost Beliefs of Northern Europe*
H. R. Ellis Davidson – *The Road to Hell*

P. T. Douglas – *Ancient Scandinavia: An Archaeological History from the First Humans to the Vikings*
G. Dumézil – *Gods of the Ancient Northmen*
P. Glob – *The Bog People: Iron-Age Man Preserved*
J. Grimm – *Teutonic Mythology*
R. North – *Heathen Gods in Old English Literature*
J. Simpson – *Everyday Life in the Viking Age*
C. Tacitus – *Germania*

Greeks and Romans

W. R. Biers – *The Archaeology of Greece*
R. Buxton – *The Complete World of Greek Mythology*
T. H. Carpenter – *Art and Myth in Ancient Greece*
G. Dumézil – *Archaic Roman Religion*
E. Gibbon – *The Decline and Fall of Roman Empire*
A. Goldsworthy – *The Complete Roman Army*
A. Goldsworthy – *The Punic Wars*
Homer – *The Iliad*
Homer – *The Odyssey*
L. Johnsen – *Lost Masters: Sages of Ancient Greece*
Polybius – *Histories*
G. Suetonius – *On Famous Men*
G. Suetonius – *The Twelve Caesars*
T. Livy – *History of Rome*
R. W. Winks – *The Ancient Mediterranean World*

Philosophy/Religion

Aristotle – *Nicomachean Ethics*
Confucius – *Analects*
D. P. Acharya – *The Dharma Manifesto*
D. P. Acharya – *Sanatana Dharma: The Eternal Natural Way*
Epictetus – *Discourses*
M. Eliade – *Patterns in Comparative Religion*
J. Evola – *Doctrine of Awakening*
J. Evola – *Meditations on the Peaks*
J. Evola – *The Metaphysics of War*
J. Evola – *The Mystery of Grail*
J. Evola – *Revolt Against the Modern World*
J. Evola – *Ride the Tiger*
D. Frawley – *The Art and Science of Vedic Counseling*
D. Frawley – *Ayurveda and the Mind*

D. Frawley – *Vedantic Meditation*
R. Guénon – *Crisis of the Modern World*
R. Guénon – *Introduction to the Study of the Hindu doctrines*
R. Guénon – *The Reign of Quantity and the Signs of the Times*
R. Guénon – *Spiritual Authority and Temporal Power*
S. Kierkegaard – *Either/Or*
S. Kierkegaard – *Fear and Trembling*
S. Kierkegaard – *The Sickness Unto Death*
Krishna – *The Bhagavad Gita*
The Laws of Manu
Marcus Aurelius – *Meditations*
F. Nietzsche – *Beyond Good and Evil*
F. Nietzsche – *The Birth of Tragedy*
F. Nietzsche – *Thus Spoke Zarathustra*
Plato – *Apology*
Plato – *Phaedo*
Plato – *The Republic*
Plato – *Symposium*
Plato – *Timaeus*
Plotinus – *The Enneads*
Seneca – *Moral Epistles*
Sun Tzu – *The Art of War*
The Upanishads

RECOMMENDED VISUAL ART

The following is a list of painters, sculptors, illustrators, and photographers, whose highly imaginative works can inspire my readers.

Contemporary Artists

Chris Achilleos
Alessia Brusco
Daria Endresen
Rob Gonsalves
John Howe
Ronja Irving
Vsevolod Ivanov
Alan Lee
Jennifer Hrabota Lesser
Laura Makabresku
Eleni Maragaki
Sergei Marshennikov

Ted Nasmith

Historical Artists

Ivan Aivazovsky
Sophie Gengembre Anderson
Albrecht Altdorfer
Peter Nicolai Arbo
James Archer
John Bauer
Albert Bierstadt
Ivan Bilibin
Nils Blommér
Arnold Böcklin
Sandro Botticelli
William-Adolphe Bouguereau
Frank Bramley
Arno Breker
Hans Andersen Brendekilde
John Brett
Edward Burne-Jones
Gaston Bussière
Julia Margaret Cameron
Carl Gustav Carus
Józef Chełmoński
Galileo Chini
John Collier
Léon Comerre
Walter Crane
Johan Christian Dahl
Evelyn De Morgan
Ludwig Dettmann
Frank Dicksee
Karl Wilhelm Diefenbach
Emil Doepler
Gustav Doré
Dankvart Dreyer
John Duncan
Albrecht Dürer
Erich Erler
Ludwig Fahrenkrog
Stanhope Alexander Forbes
Caspar David Friedrich

Victor Gabriel Gilbert
Heinrich Gogarten
John Atkinson Grimshaw
Hans Gude
Arthur Hacker
Anton Hansch
Hermann Hendrich
Arthur Hughes
Edward Robert Hughes
Talbot Hughes
William Holman Hunt
Johann Jungblut
Dragoš Kalajić
Theodor Kittelsen
Gustav Klimt
Otto Albert Koch
Reinhold Kukla
Carl Larsson
Ferdinand Leeke
Edmund Blair Leighton
Bruno Liljefors
Évariste Vital Luminais
Johan Thomas Lundbye
Rene Magritte
Horatio McCulloch
John Everett Millais
Walter Moras
Gustave Moreau
Hanna Pauli
Phidias
Maximilian Pirner
Ilya Repin
Nicholas Roerich
Dante Gabriel Rossetti
Ferdynand Ruszczyc
Jakub Schikaneder
Carlos Schwabe
Ivan Shishkin
Alfons Siber
Sidney Sime
Otto Sinding
Carl Spitzweg
Adolf Stademann

John Stanhope
Pelle Swedlund
Adolph Tidemand
Johannes Vermeer
Heinrich Vogeler
Julius von Klever
Franz von Stuck
John William Waterhouse
Jan Hendrik Weissenbruch
Dagfin Werenskiold
Gustav Wertheimer
Thomas Worthington Whittredge
Alfred Wierusz-Kowalski
Mårten Eskil Winge
Leon Wyczółkowski

RECOMMENDED MUSIC

The following is my personal list of music albums well worth listening to. The intention of this selection is to familiarize my readers with a wide array of various compositions and songs that evoke feelings of nostalgia for the past and put one in a more meditative and relaxed mood. The emphasis is placed upon folk and medieval music from different parts of Europe.

Alan Stivell – *Celtic Symphony* [Celtic Folk Rock]
Alan Stivell – *Chemins de terre* [Celtic Folk]
Alan Stivell – *E Langonedd* [Celtic Folk]
Alan Stivell – *Legend* [Celtic Folk]
Alan Stivell – *Renaissance of the Celtic Harp* [Celtic Folk]
Alan Stivell – *The Mist of Avalon* [Celtic Folk Rock]
Backworld – *Anthems From the Pleasure Park* [Neofolk]
Biosphere – *Substrata* [Ambient]
Blood Axis – *The Gospel of Inhumanity* [Neofolk]
Brendan Perry – *Ark* [Ethereal]
Brian Eno – *Ambient 1: Music for Airports* [Ambient]
Brian Eno – *Ambient 2: The Plateaux of Mirror* [Ambient]
Brian Eno – *Apollo* [Ambient]
Brian Eno – *Discreet Music* [Ambient]
Camerata Mediolanense – *Campo di Marte* [Neoclassical/Martial Industrial]
Camerata Mediolanense – *Madrigali* [Neoclassical/Martial Industrial]
Camerata Mediolanense – *Musica Reservata* [Neoclassical/Martial

Industrial]
Camerata Mediolanense – *Vertute, Honor, Bellezza* [Neoclassical/Martial Industrial]
Capercaillie – *Delirium* [Celtic Folk Rock]
Current 93 – *All the Pretty Little Horses* [Neofolk]
Current 93 – *Soft Black Stars* [Neofolk]
Current 93 – *Thunder Perfect Mind* [Neofolk]
Daemonia Nymphe – *Daemonia Nymphe* [Ancient Greek Music]
Dead Can Dance – *Aion* [Neoclassical Darkwave]
Dead Can Dance – *Anastasis* [World Music]
Dead Can Dance – *Dead Can Dance* [Gothic Rock]
Dead Can Dance – *Dionysus* [World Music]
Dead Can Dance – *Spiritchaser* [World Music]
Dead Can Dance – *The Serpent's Egg* [Neoclassical Darkwave]
Dead Can Dance – *Within the Realm of a Dying Sun* [Neoclassical Darkwave]
Drudkh – *Songs of Grief and Solitude* [Ukrainian Folk]
Eberhard Weber – *Pendulum* [Meditative Jazz]
Eivør Pálsdóttir – *Bridges* [Nordic Folk Pop]
Eivør Pálsdóttir – *Room* [Nordic Folk Pop]
Eivør Pálsdóttir – *Slør* [Nordic Folk Pop]
Ensemble Kérylos – *Musique de l'antiquité grecque* [Ancient Greek Music]
Ensemble Mare Balticum – *Ice and Longboats: Ancient Music of Scandinavia* [Ancient Nordic Music]
Enya – *The Celts* [Ambient]
Estampie – *Musik von Troubadours und Flagellanten* [Medieval Music]
Estampie – *Zeit und Vergänglichkeit im Mittelalter* [Medieval Music]
Forndom – *Dauðra Dura* [Nordic Folk]
Gjallarhorn – *Ranarop* [Nordic Folk]
Harold Budd – *Lovely Thunder* [Ambient]
Harold Budd – *The Pearl* [Ambient]
Harold Budd – *The White Arcades* [Ambient]
Hedningarna – *Hedningarna* [Nordic Folk]
Hendinganra – *Trä* [Nordic Folk]
Horslips – *The Book of Invasions* [Celtic Progressive Folk Rock]
Horslips – *The Táin* [Celtic Progressive Folk Rock]
Irene Papas & Vangelis – *Odes* [Greek Folk]
Ivar Bjørnson & Einar Selvik – *Hugsjá* [Nordic Folk]
Joculatores Upsaliensis – *Skogen, flickan och flaskan* [Medieval/Renaissance Folk]
Kalenda Maya – *Medieval and Renaissance Music* [Medieval/Renaissance Folk]

Kalenda Maya – *Norske Middelalderballader* [Medieval Folk]
Krauka – *Bylur* [Nordic Folk]
Krauka – *Stiklur* [Nordic Folk]
Lisa Gerrard – *Departum* [Ethereal]
Loreena McKennit – *Elemental* [Celtic Folk]
Loreena McKennit – *Parallel Dreams* [Celtic Folk]
Loreena McKennit – *The Visit* [Celtic Folk]
Loreena McKennit – *To Drive the Cold Wind Away* [Celtic Folk]
Musica Sveciae – *The Sounds of Prehistoric Scandinavia* [Ancient Nordic Music]
Myrkur – *Mausoleum* [Nordic Folk]
Of the Wand & the Moon – *The Lone Descent* [Neofolk]
Popol Vuh – *Brüder des Schattens – Söhne des Lichts* [Ambient]
Popol Vuh – *Die Nacht der Seele* [Ambient]
Popol Vuh – *Hosianna Mantra* [Devotional Music]
Popol Vuh – *In den Gärten Pharaos* [Krautrock]
Popol Vuh – *Nosferatu* [Ambient]
Tangerine Dream – *Phaedra* [Electronic Music]
Tangerine Dream – *Poland* [Electronic Music]
Tangerine Dream – *Rubycon* [Electronic Music]
Tangerine Dream – *Stratosfear* [Electronic Music]
Tangerine Dream – *Tangram* [Electronic Music]
Torulf – *Västerled* [Nordic Tribal Ambient]
Ulver – *Teachings in Silence* [Ambient]
Ulver – *The Norwegian National Opera* [Electronic Music]
Wardruna – *Runaljod - gap var Ginnunga* [Nordic Folk]
Wardruna – *Runaljod - Ragnarok* [Nordic Folk]
Wardruna – *Runaljod - Yggdrasil* [Nordic Folk]
Wolcensmen – *Songs From the Fyrgen* [Anglo-Saxon Folk]
Wolcensmen – *Songs From the Mere* [Anglo-Saxon Folk]

RECOMMENDED FILMS

The following is a list of recommended films with philosophical, religious, historical, and artistic themes which are relevant to the content of this book. Note that in many cases a recommendation does not necessarily imply endorsement of the entire film.

M. Antonioni – *Red Desert*
G. Axel – *Hagbard and Signe*
F. Baldi – *Massacre in the Black Forest*
I. Bergman – *The Hour of the Wolf*

I. Bergman – *The Virgin Spring*
I. Bergman – *The Seventh Seal*
R. Bresson – *Lancelot of the Lake*
M. Cacoyannis – *Electra*
M. Cacoyannis – *Iphigenia*
Arnaud des Pallières – *Michael Kohlhaas*
C. T. Dreyer – *Day of Wrath*
C. T. Dreyer – *Ordet*
S. Eisenstein – *Alexander Nevsky*
G. Ferroni – *Coriolanus*
R. Fleischer – *The Vikings*
P. Flinth – *Eye of the Eagle*
R. Fricke – *Baraka*
R. Fricke – *Chronos*
R. Fricke – *Samsara*
Á. Guðmundsson – *Outlaw: The Saga of Gisli*
S. Gunnarsson – *Beowulf & Grendel*
H. Gunnlaugsson – *When the Raven Flies*
A. Harvey – *The Lion in Winter*
W. Herzog – *Aguirre*
W. Herzog – *The Enigma of Kaspar Hauser*
W. Herzog – *Fitzcarraldo*
W. Herzog – *Heart of Glass*
W. Herzog – *Nosferatu*
G. Hessler – *The Golden Voyage of Sindbad*
M. Kobayashi – *Harakiri*
S. Kubrick – *Spartacus*
A. Kurosawa – *Dersu Uzala*
A. Kurosawa – *Ran*
A. Kurosawa – *Rashomon*
A. Kurosawa – *Seven Samurai*
A. Kurosawa – *Throne of Blood*
F. Lang – *Die Nibelungen*
S. Parajanov – *The Colour of Pomegranates*
S. Parajanov – *The Legend of Suram Fortress*
S. Parajanov – *Shadows of Forgotten Ancestors*
A. Tarkovsky – *Andrei Rublev*
A. Tarkovsky – *Nostalghia*
A. Tarkovsky – *Solaris*
A. Tarkovsky – *Stalker*
T. Vinterberg – *Festen*
F. Vláčil – *Marketa Lazarová*

Printed in Great Britain
by Amazon